D0559888

Democracy at work

International series on the quality of working life

Vol. 2

Democracy at work

The report of the Norwegian industrial democracy program

Fred Emery and Einar Thorsrud
Centre for Continuing Education ANU, Canberra
Professor of Social Psychology, University of Oslo

In co-operation with
Per H. Engelstad,
Jon Gulowsen
Thoralf Qale

Martinus Nijhoff Social Sciences Division
Leiden 1976

ISBN 90 207 0633 0

Printed by Mennen, Asten, the Netherlands.

Contents

Introduction

It is with mixed feelings that we write this introduction. Major parts of the book first appeared in 1970, in Norwegian (Thorsrud and Emery, 1970). We promised an early English edition but found ourselves at opposite ends of the world, both giving first priority to opening up development projects in new areas. In a way, publication has been a temporary victim of our own theory of diffusing social change.

The delay has been embarrassing but at least we have had the reassuring knowledge that the field experiments and experiences are as relevant today as they were then and relevant to a now much wider English speaking audience.

The four field experiments reported here all arose from the Norwegian Industrial Democracy Project (the ID project).

Several features of this project were quite unique for the social science world of the 1960s.

Why did the concept *Industrial Democracy* become central in this project? The answer is very simple. It was the problem area of industrial democracy that we, as social scientists, were invited to study and to help to do something about. We were given ample opportunity in collaboration with the sponsors, to redefine the alternative meanings of industrial democracy and we were convinced that the key concept was meaningful enough for those involved. It might also lead them to act if alternative solutions became available. This led to the planning of two phases of research and development, – the first concentrating on the experiences gained with formal systems of participation through representative arrangements (Emery and Thorsrud, 1964). The second dealt with field experiments and socio-technical changes to improve the concrete conditions for direct, participative industrial democracy.

First and foremost the ID project aimed at the development and testing of *alternative organizational forms and their impacts upon employee partici-*

pation on different levels of companies. Major emphasis was placed on the concrete conditions for personal participation, including technological factors structuring the tasks, the work roles and the wider organizational environment of workers. The project could not be limited to the level of the workers, since major changes in any work system would affect all levels of an organization. But it seemed important to focus on the workers' level for two reasons. First: it is on this level that the lack of participation and involvement is most widespread. Second: jobs are currently designed on workers' level in such a way that it is very difficult to achieve basic changes in the control systems and in participative relationships on supervisory and other levels. Jobs are often so narrow and meaningless that supervisors and higher levels of management are sucked into control and co-ordination of details. This will in itself cause frustration rather than participation and there will be little time for constructive long term improvement.

'*Semi-autonomous work groups*' came to be an important aspect of our explorations of alternative forms of organization. The individual has his limitations as a building block in organizational design for technological reasons. Process control and information handling can not be dealt with entirely on an individual basis. There were also a number of psychological and social reasons for exploring the potential usefulness of autonomous groups in this particular context. Team work has always been an important part of traditional western work culture. Theoretical reasons for considering groups as important for participation have been given in a series of studies following Lewin's early experiments with group climate. (Lewin, 1938).

A major feature of the ID project has been the active engagement of researchers in social change. With the present rate of change in technology as well as in the social aspects of industrial life any alternative structure of organization might be obsolete almost before it could be established. The answer to this dilemma might be to build a great deal of *re*organizational ability into the organizations themselves. So the ID project has become an attempt to establish a self-sustaining process of organizational learning.

In what respect then was the ID project different from other change projects? It was related to the tradition initiated by Kurt Lewin in Berlin, pre 1933 and developed further in the US in 1950-60 by The Institute for Social Research at the University of Michigan (Mann, F., 1957). It was strongly influenced by the work done during the fifties by the Tavistock Institute of Human Relations in England (Trist, 1958). But the ID project was different from the Michigan and Tavistock studies because the institutional involvement went far beyond that of a single project in one or a few work organizations. Within the Norwegian cultural framework it was possible in the 1960s to establish a set of starting conditions *for large scale social change over a period of at least ten years*. The strategy of change was based on leadership and support from Trade Unions, the Employers Association and gradually from government. The role of successive field experiments as a way of testing and demonstrating new principles of organization was crucial in our strategy. It included four major steps; information, involvement, commitment and joint social action. This stepwise strategy had a parallel in agricultural change programmes (Emery and Oeser, 1958).

A programme of this size and time perspective demanded research resources beyond what was available in Norway. The collaboration with the Tavistock group was vital. Links to Sweden, Holland and the US became important.

The relations established between the researchers and the researched can be classified according to Churchman and Emery (1966), who distinguished three major roles for social scientists working with organizations; namely the academic, the servant, and the collaborative roles. The research roles of the ID project clearly fall in the third category. The project satisfies two basic conditions stated by Churchman and Emery, namely, first, agreement that the research will be guided by some set of values that include the values of the researcher and the researched, and secondly, some body able to sanction this over-riding set of values. A sanctioning body, the Joint Research Committee, was set up by the Trade Union Council and the Employers' Association, the two institutions which shared the financing of the project until Government came in on a tri-partite basis. The value problems can perhaps best be considered when we have reported the cumulative research work. Only one point should be made clear in advance. The researchers as well as the collaborating organizations and institutions had to accept that their own value structure as well as that of anybody else to be involved in the ID project might change as the project went on. It was clear that this was a condition for some basic alternatives to be realised in terms of democratization. In other words; the project itself might generate new values, and it would have to affect the power structure if results of some importance were to be achieved in practice. For this reason, it was necessary at every major step to let those directly involved participate actively in formulation of the goals of their project. They had to agree on conditions to be changed and the criteria to be used in evaluating the outcome of whatever changes might be achieved. (For further discussion of our research strategies see Chapter 1.)

The primary focus of the studies was organization at the work-face. For theoretical guidance we started from the work done on sociotechnical systems and job redesign. (Trist and Bamforth, 1951, Rice 1958, Davis 1955-1957, Emery 1959). These principles are outlined in the main text, as are the relevant theoretical developments we were able to make during our work.

Each of the work faces was embodied in a company organization, not a laboratory. A theoretical framework was needed to understand the organizational factors impinging on the experiments, the processes controlling diffusion, and the environmental factors constraining both organizational processes. This framework was drawn in particular from Selznick (1949) and from open system and system-environment concepts. (Emery and Trist, 1960, Emery 1963a, b.) The organizational principles that most influenced our approach to our practical affairs were as follows:

1. 'The *goals* of an organization can be understood as special forms of interdependence between the enterprise and its environment. (The interdependence is represented in terms of easily measured inputs and outputs on the one hand, e.g. raw materials or outputs of certain products, and in much more intangible interdependencies like the common values of collaborative organizations.)
2. The enterprise as an open system will strive for a *steady state* in relation to its environment by maintaining a tolerable rate of progress toward its objectives and constancy of direction despite changes in the environment or the organization.
3. The *variations* in the input and output markets that can be coped with by the organization in a complex environment depend on the *flexibility* of its technology and on the degree of *self regulation* of its component parts. A shared sense of commitment to a *mission* and a *distinctive competence* will also increase the ability of the enterprise to cope with variations in its environment.
4. A steady state for an organization cannot be achieved by any finite combination of regulatory devices or mechanisms that are aimed at achieving a steady state for some partial aspect of the system. *Leadership* and *commitment* of members are basic conditions for maintaining a steady state. Goals and values directing the activities of members must be clearly enough defined to maintain uni-directedness and growth. Commitment of members must be strong enough for them to respond to

external challenges by self regulation of their efforts. (The impact of regulatory mechanisms in an enterprise such as cost control, computerized planning etc. must be viewed in terms of their contribution to self-regulation.) The measure of the efficiency of self-regulation, of whether the system is healthy, is to be found in the capability of the enterprise to fulfill the tasks arising from its mission. (A good record of performance, e.g. high profits, would not in itself exclude the possibility that potential capacity had in fact been reduced.)

5. The task of management is primarily governed by the need to match constantly the actual and potential capacities of the enterprise to the actual and potential requirements of the environment. In other words, the *primary task of management is the boundary control* of the enterprise. In so far as the manager has to co-ordinate internal variances in the organization he is distracted from his primary task.
6. An enterprise can achieve the conditions for steady state only if it allows to its members a measure of *autonomy* and *selective interdependence*. The autonomy of members enabling them to make choices and to exercise control over their own work situation will tend to increase their commitment. Internal co-ordination of organizational components through self regulation will put limitations on autonomy of individuals and consequently on their commitment. These limitations can be at least partly overcome by allowing selective interdependence to members of an organization. This is clearly illustrated by the way professionals relate to each other in the context of their organizations. It is less clear in the case of rank and file workers.' (Emery, 1963a).

We stress that these were theoretical guidelines or principles. They suggested ways of looking at things and sometimes reminded us to look at aspects we had ignored. They informed discussion within the research team and with some of our other professional colleagues. They were *not* the currency of our exchanges with workers and management.

These are the main points we wish to make about the background of the studies reported herein.

Since the studies were completed many closely related developments have taken place. Even though we have been involved in many of these developments this is no place to attempt a comprehensive review. We will just indicate what we think has been significant and refer the reader to relevant sources of further information.

The most striking development has been the explosion of similar reorganizations of work since 1969. First, and most notably, in Sweden but then elsewhere in western countries (Jenkins, 1972 and O'Toole, 1973). Within Norway applications have spread slowly but very steadily in industry and into white-collar work; moved rapidly into shipping (Roggema and Thorsrud, 1974) and most recently into education (WR1, 1974).

Less public, but probably of equal significance for the near future, have beenthe developments in understanding the processes of diffusion.

1. For diffusion in large organizations there was a recognized need for an explicit company philosophy for the management of human recources. Without this changes in parts of an organization were at risk from variations in philosophy of individual managers. (Hill, 1970).
2. Over the series of studies we report the reader will notice that our role as experts was becoming less central to initiating and sustaining change. In retrospect we can see that we were slow to comprehend this shift. The Swedish 'do-it-yourself' developments brought it very much to our awareness. It also made us seriously consider whether, in the newly emerging social climate of the late sixties, our part as experts had contributed to the partial encapsulation, sealing-off, that we had seen at some of the experimental sites (Herbst, 1974). In response to this a systematic procedure has begun to emerge for relegating the expert more to the background and for involving people in the re-design of their own workplaces. (Emery and Emery, 1974)

It is no coincidence that the more direct and down to earth approach developed in Australia in the early seventies. A 'grass root' approach was both more possible and more relevant then than it would have been in Scandinavia in the early sixties.

A similar need for policy clarification on the Asian side has been equally important and even more difficult to achieve. This has been the case particularly where a centralized bureaucratic structure on the one side has for some time reinforced the same type of structure on the other, the trade union side.

Theoretical developments within the socio-technical framework are best reflected in Herbst (1974): a shift in the broader frame-of-reference in Emery (1974 b). The shift seems to have occurred rather as follows. We earlier believed that the 'scientific management' school had something to their claim that their notions of organization flowed naturally from the nature of modern technological systems to give 'a machine theory of organization'. With each detailed sociotechnical study from 1950 on, it became clearer that there was always some 'organizational choice' (Trist

1963). Nevertheless, we started the Norwegian project with the cautious assumption that each major technology would have to be studied to identify its degrees of freedom. We got involved in the mid sixties with the process industry cases (and with the Shell, UK refineries, Hill, 1972). We were increasingly impressed by lack of really significant differences in technological constraints on organizational choice. Our interpretation was that with increasing instrumentation and automation the technical interface with the workers was approaching a common denominator of information technology. Subsequent experience with clerical and professional work suggested something more profound. It seemed that there was 'The Myth of the Machine'. (Mumford, 1967). The organizational theory opposing ours was not 'a machine theory of organization' but a general theory of bureaucracy (Emery, 1974 a). The implications were fairly profound. In the first and older perspective our task was to prove for each technology that organizational choice was possible; as each new technology emerged our task was on again. In the second perspective, the relevance of our approach could be established by asking a single question, 'is management necessary to the organization?' If the answer is yes, then, regardless of technology, some degree of self-management of groups of members is possible. Socio-technical theory does not thereby go out of the door. To go from what is organizationally possible to what is viable one must answer such critical questions as 'what groups should be formed around what tasks'; 'how *semi*-autonomous', (Gullowsen, 1971), 'what degree of *multi*-skilling is necessary'. These questions can be answered only by some form of socio-technical analysis in each practical instance. The answers will depend on both technical matters and whether the people are able and willing to manage some part of their activities.

It seems appropriate now to turn to some practical things that have shaped this book and its emergence.

This is not a polished piece of writing. The field sites we describe have already been visited by more people than probably will read this book in the next year or two (managers, unionists, and social scientists from Europe, North America and Australasia). Language appears to have been no real difficulty when these visitors were seeking to learn from their counterparts in a technological environment that was common to them. We have tried to put the experiences of these sites into words that will enable people to grasp something of what happened without visiting, without being managers or workers. To exacerbate the difficulties of communication we have thrown our texts backwards and forward between English and Norwegian for some twelve years. Our resulting form is sometimes a little odd, like that of a steam-driven barque. Our apologies. Our alternative was a few more years to publication.

Lastly, we did not come into this venture thoroughly cast and well-honed from our many years in psychology. The scientific threads we were following were very thin red threads; fortunately they were threads woven by people with the hearts and minds of Kurt Lewin and Eric Trist. The very notion of scientifically tackling a nation's policy about the use of human beings in 1961 quite literally evoked unbelieving mirth from even senior colleagues at the Tavistock – a leading international centre for action research.

The development of a research team that could work in industry in the way and with the concepts we have outlined was a little saga of its own. When we started there was a marked lack of social scientists willing or able to help. However, a number of young Norwegian engineers were very concerned about the human side of their profession and prepared to re-orient their careers to the objectives of the program. A program of combined postgraduate studies and field work was organised with K. Holt and T. J. Hegland of the Department of Industrial Management, Technical University of Norway. Julius Marek came over from the Tavistock to support the academic side. Philip G. Herbst, after many years in the Tavistock's mining project was already present as a senior adviser to the project. Under those circumstances the experiments at the Spigerwerket and Hunsfos had more of an academic learning atmosphere than we would have ideally liked. The upshot for the project, however, was that the penultimate drafts of three of the chapters in this book were prepared by early graduates of the course. These are Per H. Engelstad, John Gulowsen and Lars Ødegaard (later joined by Thoralf Qvale), site research officers for the Hunsfos, Norsk Hydro and Nøbø, respectively. Knut Lange was site officer for the wire-drawing experiment. (Under the immediate guidance of Julius Marek.)

So many people helped with this project that it would be futile to try to list them. Two men above all epitomise the spirit afoot in Norway in those years that made the thing possible – Martin Siem (from the Employers' side) and Tor Aspengren (from the Union side). We think that from our reference to these two men our other friends will readily recognise who amongst them we are especially indebted to.

With considerable feeling we also record our appreciation of the strain carried by our families and also our staff members. For them it must have felt that the project would never end; that we were too dedicated and too demanding, and that we were never at home or office.

1. The socio-political background and the basic ideas of the Industrial Democracy Project

For the opening years of the sixties industrial and trade union leaders were very concerned with finding new ways of sustaining industrial growth. The rationalization movement had strengthened industry's influence during the years of reconstruction after World War II but had also started to show its shortcomings. The restrictions it imposed on individual freedom and creativity and its negative impact on social life in the workplace had started to draw heavy criticism.

At the same time Norway was confronted with the possibility of joining the European Common Market and hence losing the protective barriers which helped many industries to succeed in the home market. These economic concerns and the growing restlessness of the left-wing of the then ruling Labour Party combined to arouse a strong interest in the ever-nagging debate about the impersonal, authoritarian-dependency culture that is so characteristic of large-scale modern industry. This culture was clearly in conflict with the autonomous, self-reliant traditions of Norwegian society. This social debate was, we found, a very real debate. Norway had entered late into industrialisation and its traditional culture had not been shattered by those things, such as child labour and official violence, which marked the industrialisation of the UK and later of the USA. The homogeneity of the Norwegian nation and its culture came intact through the phase of industrialisation. The entrepreneurs and organisers of industry achieved their goals of industrial growth through continuous accommodation to the culture. This accommodation is clearly manifested in the early emergence of social welfare provisions, legal trade unionism and legal recognition of negotiated labour agreements. It is further illustrated by the way the industrial working day has been structured around the traditional meal pattern with the main meal in mid-afternoon, and by some of the peculiar shift systems that have been devised to enable a considerable part of the workforce to continue as part-time farmers or fishermen or in any case to work by 'skippertak', by spurts rather than always to follow the regular machine-like pace preferred by most industrial organisers.

More overtly the pressures on industry to accommodate had resulted in a 1948 law establishing workers' representatives on the boards of industries owned or partly owned by the Government. At about the same time, the negotiated Common Agreement made it compulsory for industries to set up Joint Production Committees. Now, in the early sixties, leaders in industry, the unions and in politics felt that something had to be done to raise the level of individual participation in industry.

In late 1961 the Trade Unions Council (LO) and the National Confederation of Employers (NAF) each set up committees to study problems of industrial democracy. Both committees felt that some of these problems required social scientific research. In 1962 the Institute for Industrial Social Research in Trondheim was asked to undertake this. In their turn the Institute sought and obtained the professional collaboration of the Tavistock Institute of Human Relations.

The NAF and LO then took the unprecedented step of establishing a Joint Committee on Research. This had never been done before because neither body would publicly recognise that they had any joint interests apart from those reflected in their joint acceptance of the Labour Laws. The Joint Committee co-ordinated their interests in social scientific research, provided the necessary sanctioning of the project, and facilitated communication and contact with the research team.[1]

In their first two meetings, in 1962, the Joint Committee agreed that their interests would be met by a two-pronged research programme:

1. a study of existing Norwegian and foreign experience with mechanisms that allow formally for employee representation at top management level; (Thorsrud and Emery, 1964)
2. a study of the roots of industrial democracy in the condition of personal participation in the work place.

The Joint Committee and the research team agreed at these early meetings that the second line of research, the study of personal participation, was of basic interest. On existing evidence, it appeared that the manner in which employees participate in the work life of their companies was critical for the

1. For the first year the Project was financed 50-50 by the LO and NAF. After that the Government entered as a silent partner, paying one-third. The new Labour Agreement negotiated by LO and NAF in 1966 formally institutionalised a new joint committee and the Government undertook to meet all of the financial requirements.

use they make of formal mechanisms for representation and consultation, for their apathy or constructive interest, and their job satisfaction. The bulk of this evidence suggested that the more the individual was enabled to exercise control over his task, and to relate his efforts to those of his fellows, the more likely was he to accept a positive commitment to doing a good job. This positive commitment shows in a number of ways, not the least of which is the release of that personal initiative and creativity which is the basis of a democratic climate. Only when these conditions exist could we expect democratic representative structures to be evolved that are appropriate to the very real restraints that exist in industry. And only then could we expect these institutions to be used effectively by those whom they are supposed to serve. However, there was no single technique that seemed applicable in all industrial conditions to raise the level of individual participation. Thus, while job enlargement or job enrichment had proved effective in some conditions, it might be inappropriate in others, and certainly too limited to serve the objectives of the ID project. Development of autonomous work groups had been effective in some conditions but was unproven over a great range of others. In most cases increased skills seemed to be essential but in some only small changes seemed called for. The important point seemed to be that the kind of changes required were likely to be related to the kind of technology involved and the existing social setting. Any general principles for redesign of jobs in the desired direction would probably have to be translated for each major kind of technology and each translation empirically tested, and, if effective, demonstrated.[2] With these views in mind, the Joint Committee considered the different sectors of industry and decided that a start should be made in two sectors – metal manufacturing and pulp and paper. These were considered to be the most strategic sectors of the Norwegian economy, and hence had top priority. They would also present basically different technological settings. (Shipping was considered to be a special case and was not covered by the ID project before 1967.)

The next problem was to find, within each sector, a suitable plant for study.

If this line of research was to bear fruit, it was considered necessary that the researchers should not only study existing experience, but also experimentally modify the conditions of personal participation and measure the

2. By 1966 we believed that 'as work processes became automated and computerized the traditional differences tend to disappear and the common problem is that of achieving higher personal participation in systems for information handling and processing.' For our views in 1974 refer to the Introduction.

resulting changes in such things as job satisfaction – dissatisfaction, apathy – constructive interest, communication level, productivity, stability and growth.

It was explicitly agreed that experiments along these lines should be conducted in such a way that:

1. the management and employees who agreed to carry out experimental modifications of existing practices should by fully informed at all stages of what was going on and of what was proposed for the next steps. They should at all times feel free to insist on modification or cessation of the experiments after each step. Furthermore there should be no communication of *findings* to outsiders without their approval;
2. any emergent lessons should be such as could be readily evaluated by the interested parties;
3. there should be some inducement to learn from these lessons, not only for the company directly concerned in an experiment but also for other companies.[3]

In order that there should be a widespread willingness to learn from any emergent lessons, it was considered essential that the relevant national leaders in management and the trade unions should be:

1. informed beforehand of what was being undertaken;
2. agreed beforehand on what changes in the workplace would be relevant to their notions of industrial democracy;
3. agreed that the plants within which the experiments are carried out were not so unusual as to nullify the relevance to others of the results.

As a preliminary step toward meeting these conditions the members of the Joint Committee discussed our proposals for research with management and trade union leaders in the chosen industrial sectors and selected a short list of plants that they regarded as satisfactorily representative of their industry. These plants were fairly representative with respect to factors that are difficult to vary at will, e.g. technology, labour force, capital and, to some extent, market, even though they were not necessarily representative with respect to matters that are up to management and labour to change. The managers of the short-listed plants were all men who were highly respected in their industry and likely to influence others by their example. The researchers

3. In practice we also found it desirable to make each step in the change process as small as possible and to seek commitment only to each small step in turn.

sought to find within each short list one plant that was willing to co-operate, and had in the past *shown an ability to handle its management-labour relations in a progressive fashion.* It was then up to the researchers to establish, with the management and employees of that plant, the conditions for experimentation that best secured and protected everyone's interests. All such arrangements, whether at plant level or sector level, were matters on which we sought the approval of the Joint NAF/LO Committee because they were sponsoring and financing the research for national interests, and hence had to assure for themselves that these interests are not being sacrificed to strictly local interests.

The goals set up by LO and NAF, and readily accepted by us, were basically to lessen alienation in work of the person from his productive activity[4] and hence release human resources. There were of course restraints on the pursuit of these objectives. The most obvious constraints concerned profitability and productivity. Neither party was willing to sacrifice the rising standards of living that were based on profitability and productivity, although both parties expressed willingness to seek changes that would reduce alienation even if they did not increase productivity. There were indications of some less obvious contraints, e.g. the feeling that work was unavoidably punishment, that ordinary people needed to be under paternal guidance (Protestant ethic?). Thus we were expected to prove that the lessening of alienation would neither encourage self-indulgence nor weaken social discipline. Furthermore, there were constraints on the management and union in their desire that the implementation should not shame persons for having acted badly in the past, nor put leaders in positions where they would be exposed to envy and ridicule. We were not able to pre-judge the importance of these constraints but we certainly did not expect the 'law of Jante' to be a dead letter in present day Norwegian culture.[5] We expected other constraints in the minds of the workers, in particular, that they would tend 'to prefer the devil they knew to one they didn't know.' We were later to be rather surprised to find the extent to which existing job specifications had become a complex system of defence against managerial pressures, and the vigour with which individuals would fight, even against their fellows, for

4. There was a small but vociferous element in Norwegian politics pressing for political measures of nationalisation or board representation to lessen that aspect of alienation due to the separation of the worker from the product of his work. The objectives of this phase of the project did not include this aspect. Phase A had concerned itself with worker directorships and 'workers control'.

5. This 'law' formulated by a Norwegian poet Sandemose includes rules like this: 'Thou shalt not believe thou art something more than we are.'

the positions of relative privilege that they had secured for themselves. We initially overestimated the extent to which men thought critically about the limitations of their present jobs, and we underestimated their fearful suspicions of management.

Despite the widespread and historically deep roots of alienation, we believed that there was some possible help to be gained from social scientists. The most immediate reason for these beliefs was the series of industrial experiments carried out by the Tavistock Institute of Human Relations (in British coal-mining and Indian textiles) where steps to reduce alienation had been successful in these terms. Supporting this were parallel studies that had been done in Holland and USA. A very considerable body of social scientific experience existed to define some of the principles of industrial organisation and job design which tend to reduce work alienation (Emery, 1959). It seemed very probable that employers and trade unionists could apply these principles to redesign existing jobs and design new ones to reduce alienation without loss of productivity or deterioration in the material conditions of employment.

The judgement that it is possible to design or redesign jobs in this way rests upon the evidence that men have requirements of their work other than those usually specified in a contract of employment (i.e. other than wages, hours, safety, security of tenure, etc.). The following list represents at least some of the general psychological requirements that pertain to the content of a job; to what a person needs if he is called upon to carry out in his job from hour to hour, from week to week, and from year to year:

1. The need for the content of the job to be reasonably demanding (challenging) in terms other than sheer endurance and yet providing some variety (not necessarily novelty).
2. The need for being able to learn on the job and go on learning (which imply known and appropriate standards, and knowledge of results). Again it is a question of neither too much nor too little.
3. The need for some area of decision-making that the individual can call his own.
4. The need for some minimal degree of helpfulness and recognition in the workplace.
5. The need to be able to relate what he does and what he produces to his social life.
6. The need to feel that the job leads to some sort of desirable future.

These requirements are obviously not confined to any one level of employment. Nor is it possible to meet these requirements in the same way in all work settings or for all kinds of people. Complicating matters further is the fact that these needs cannot always be judged from their conscious expression. Like *any* general psychological requirements they are subject to a wide range of vicissitudes. Thus, where there is no expectation that any of the jobs open to a person will offer much chance of learning, that person will soon learn to 'forget' such requirements.

As already indicated, these requirements, however true they may be, are too general to serve as principles for job redesign. For this purpose they need to be linked to the objective characteristics of industrial jobs. The following is the preliminary set of such principles with which these studies started. They represent the best we were able to achieve by way of generalising upon existing findings. They are not, we hope, final.

1.1. Detailed principles for the redesigning of jobs

1.1.1. At the level of the individual[6]

1. *Optimum variety of tasks* within the job. Too much variety can be inefficient for training and production as well as frustrating for the worker. However, too little can be conducive to boredom or fatigue. The optimum level would be that which allows the operator to take a rest from a high level of attention or effort on a demanding activity by working at another related but less demanding task and, conversely, allow him to stretch himself and his capacities after a period of routine activity.
2. *A meaningful pattern of tasks that gives to each job a semblance of a single overall task.* The tasks should be such that, although involving different levels of attention, degrees of effort, or kinds of skill, they are interdependent: that is, carrying out one task makes it easier to get on with the next or gives a better end result to the overall task. Given such a pattern, the worker can more easily find a method of working suitable to this requirements and can more easily relate his job to that of others.
3. *Optimum length of work cycle.* Too short a cycle means too much finishing

6. Lewin's experimental work on task demands was at the basis of these principles (Lewin 1951 and Emery 1959). However, without the counterfoil of Davis' incisive analysis of the current practices of production engineers (1955, 1957) we could not, at that stage, have so easily made the transposition from psychology laboratory to workshop.

and starting: too long a cycle makes it difficult to build up a rhythm of work.

4. *Some scope for setting standards of quantity and quality of production and a suitable feedback of knowledge of results.* Minimum standards generally have to be set by management to determine whether a worker is sufficiently trained, skilled or careful to hold the job. Workers are more likely to accept responsibility for higher standards if they have some freedom in setting them and are likely to learn from the job only if there is feedback. They can neither effectively set standards nor learn if there is not a quick enough feedback of knowledge of results.
5. *The inclusion in the job of some of the auxiliary and preparatory tasks.* The worker cannot and will not accept responsibility for matters outside his control. Insofar as the preceding criteria are met then the inclusion of such 'boundary tasks' will extend the scope of the workers' responsibility and make for involvement in the job. They will be his responsibility, not his excuses.
6. *The tasks included in the job should include some degree of care, skill, knowledge or effort that is worthy of respect in the community.*
7. *The job should make some perceivable contribution to the utility of the product for the consumer.*

1.1.2. At the group level

1. *Providing for 'interlocking' tasks, job rotation or physical proximity where there is a necessary interdependence of jobs* (for technical or psychological reasons). At a minimum this helps to sustain communication and to create mutual understanding between workers whose tasks are interdependent and thus lessens friction, recriminations and 'scape-goating'. At best, this procedure will help to create work groups that enforce standards of co-operation and mutual help.
2. *Providing for interlocking tasks, job rotation or physical proximity where the individual job entails a relatively high degree of stress.* Stress can arise from apparently simple things such as physical demands, boredom, concentration, noise, or isolation if these persist for long periods. Left to their own devices, people will become habituated but the effects of the stress will tend to be reflected in more mistakes, accidents and anger. Support from others in a similar plight tends to lessen the strain.
3. *Providing for interlocking tasks, job rotation or physical proximity where the individual jobs do not make an obvious perceivable contribution to the utility of the end product.*

4. *Where a number of jobs are linked together by interlocking tasks or job rotation they should as a group:*
   a. have some semblance of an overall task which makes a contribution to the social utility of the product;
   b. have some scope for setting standards and receiving knowledge of results;
   c. have some control over the 'boundary tasks'.

It is clearly implied in this list of principles that the redesigning of jobs leads beyond the individual jobs to the organisation of groups of workers and beyond into the revision of our notions about supervision and the organisation of support services (such as maintenance). There was reason to believe that the implications were even wider and that they would in any organisation come to be judged as a challenge to traditional management style and philosophy. The reason seemed to be that in the particular historical conditions of the growth of modern industry there had emerged a set of principles of organisation that were based on contrary notions of job design.

The distinguishing principles of this particular method of organisation are: first, the building blocks of the organisation are the individual man and his task; second, the co-ordination of tasks is as far as possible coped with by supervisory arrangements, systems of payment, etc. The almost inevitable inadequacies of these supervisory devices seems to have acted as an incentive to management to:

1. reduce the variance arising within their man-task units. To this end we find pressures towards tighter task definition, closer supervision, TWI, rating systems, piece-work systems and the like.
2. Maximise a reserve of power and authority at the top of the management structure in readiness for the unpredicted eventualities that those lower down are eventually unable to cope with. The tendency is thus to delegate only such authorities as can be precisely accounted for in behavioural terms, i.e. in terms of what is predictable, and to delegate such powers for as short a time as is possible.

Operating with these principles sets up forces which will develop into a vicious circle when conditions deviate from normal operating conditions. The more management tries to tightly control the man-task relation the greater the probability that the man will develop informal practices and informal groups to defeat these efforts. Likewise, with tighter, more explicit and more detailed, specification of their task responsibilities, men will increasingly neglect anything that does not come under the job definition, even though it would obviously improve the outcome of the work. Both of these tendencies act to increase uncontrolled variability in the system. Similarly with the operation of the second of these principles. Given that the lower levels of management also have to cope with unexpected variances (contingencies) they will in the absence of adequate delegating of power, either strive for illegitimate power, which is then not known to and not under the guidance of higher management, or will have to generate excuses to cloud over their impotence to exercise responsibility without power.

When an organisation that is being run on these principles gets into an externally induced crisis the expected response is to tighten the screws on middle management and men. The expected result, unless the crisis is shortlived, is that the degree of uncontrolled variance will increase. To which the response is to tighten up further. Each tightening up brings every level of management further down into the affairs of the level below and, by making it increasingly harder for the operators to buck the system, which they will increasingly wish to do, increases the emotional tension in management-worker relations.

The vicious circle that has been set up by trying to operate with the above two principles has not, unfortunately, stopped with efforts to intensify the social controls over individual performance. The engineering design and development of technology has, we suggest, been biased towards those technological solutions that favour fractionalisation of the task and external supervision. Sometimes this seems to have arisen from manufacturers specifying their engineering requirements in terms of a breakdown that they customarily impose upon the task (a breakdown that is more related to their managerial practices than to the natural characteristics of the task); sometimes from the engineer's own assumptions about the fallibility of man and a desire to reduce to a minimum the error that the individual can introduce into his design of a man-machine system, i.e. the engineers' desire for a 'fool-proof' system (Jordan, Chap. 12, 1968).

This 'engineering' approach to productive systems appears to be the obverse of what is implied in this research programme. In the former, the social and psychological aspects have been treated as relevant only insofar as they constitute boundary conditions of the technological system and an effort is made to reduce them to boundary constants (in part by definition of the contractual arrangements of employment). With some justice this approach has been labelled the 'Machine Theory of Organisation'. With greater justice Mumford has argued that technological design has been biased toward more ancient principles of labour control.

In the approach that we have been defining the over-riding concern is with *joint optimization* of the social and technical systems. Neither system can make its maximum contribution to the performance of the overall system unless each is optimized with respect to each other. Development of a technical system beyond the point where its operation by human beings can effectively link together its 'open ends' is self-defeating. It is equally self-defeating to develop the social system to the point where its members lose interest in linking together the open technical ends to make a productive socio-technical system.

From the above account it might seem that the process of testing and diffusing principles is too unstructured to grasp and much too dependent upon faith to be rationally controlled. However, these processes occur in all fields of human endeavour and we have considerable experience of new principles ousting old principles and these in turn being modified in the light of practice. The most systematic scientific study of these processes before 1962 had been in the spread of scientific knowledge to farmers. The innovations studied have ranged from quite specific calculable innovations such as antibiotics to general principles of animal husbandry and farm management. The key lessons have been:

1. the ability of outside scientific advisors to directly affect the diffusion process tends to be limited to their influence on the leaders. Not necessarily because of their natural ability but because it is the primary task of leaders to relate to the outside.
2. Diffusion must be firmly based on an existing power structure – cascading, as it were, from one level of leaders to the next.
3. Verbal and written communication is rarely sufficient to induce change, except at the level of the leaders.
4. Beyond the leaders, diffusion requires the force of example; to be forceful the example must be such that the other person must be able to readily identify the similarity to his own conditions and he must usually be provided with an accepted examplar.

With these lessons in mind, we considered that the appropriate strategy for the project as a whole was to:

1. Develop through discussion with national leaders some understanding of

the principles, a willingness to have them tested out, and a commitment to use their power to exploit any successful breakthroughs.

2. Establish field sites where the testing out could be done under real-life conditions. It was expected that these sites would absorb a good deal of our social scientific resources. This was not because the local people did not know their own plant operations, their own people, etc. It was because of the difficulty that people always have in seeing the familiar things in a different way. Once they are so seen, it is often equally difficult to imagine that they were ever seen otherwise. It was expected also that the local leaders at these sites would require support from the national leaders. This could not in this case extend to financial support in the event of losses being incurred but they could give reassurance about the goals that were being pursued, e.g. that the efforts at implementation were neither a disguised attempt to squeeze the workers or an attempt to undermine managerial authority.
3. Insofar as the people at these field sites gained confidence in their ability to gain real advantages from implementing these principles, it was hoped to use these as part of a wider general diffusion. It was not expected that what was done at the field sites could be simply copied by other plants. It was expected that the respect carried by the leaders at these sites would lead others to become interested in their efforts and consider more seriously having a try for themselves. As a further aid in the same direction, we wished to familiarise industrial leaders with some of the many examples where these principles were already being realised in Norwegian industry.
4. If others were tempted to follow the key examples they would require much more skilled assistance than the limited pool of social scientists could provide. Hence a critical and early step in the diffusion process was to encourage widespread debate and understanding of the principles amongst personnel officers, training officers, work study men (unions and management), consultants and industrial engineers.

Within the framework of the research project it would be necessary therefore to attend not only to the critical problem of how the individual participates in industry by reason of his daily task but also to attend to the problems of organisational change that might be expected to arise from proposals to modify the tasks and responsibilities of the individuals.

Whatever our confidence in the validity of the principles of job design, and how to further test and develop them, we were much less sure about how to create the understanding and confidence that would enable leaders in industry to try out these principles. The problem for these leaders was clearly more difficult than adopting a new type of machinery. In that case they would normally have some figures about the objective and reproducible characteristics of the machine and the environmental conditions within which these characteristics could be expected. This makes it possible to predict how it would fit their circumstances before purchasing it. In our case, however, they have only a statement of principles. Principles for social organisation and work design do not come concretised in stable, durable metals. They become part of a working environment only when they guide people's actions. Whether they are guiding people's actions can be seen only if we take into account the circumstances in which they are acting and the kind of people they are. Hence, it is not usually possible to deduce from a knowledge of the principles how they can be fitted into any concrete productive organisation. It is necessary to go through the process of trying to fit them in before one can decide whether one's own people can implement the principles in such a way as to get the results one wants in one's own plant, and market conditions. Whether they are willing and able to take or allow significant degrees of responsibility. Whether it is possible to provide them with an adequate degree of multi-skilling.

In the last analysis one must have some successful experience with implementing the principles oneself. What works for instance on an experimental farm does not immediately persuade farmers, because they must consider how it will work for a profit on their farm with their current income, credit, farm practices, time, family labour etc. If the farmers are not put-off by some obvious drawback, real or imagined, they typically start off with very tentative testing. Testing which may still be misleading because of a distorted concept of the new idea. Introduction of a change that requires people to undo decades of experience will probably not be testable in the sort of time span that will test out a new machine or even a new technology. Bureaucratization of work, as T & M, O & M, or assembly line, has been the almost unchallengeable master of organisational theory for the past seven decades.

2. Short summary of the field experiments

2.1. Christiana Spigerverk experiment, in the wire drawing industry

This experiment shows that workers on the shop floor, with the help of outside action researchers and the backing of their shop stewards and plant management could effectively reorganize their work. They changed from one man/one machine fragmented jobs, payed on time and motion studied piece rates, to a group system of work. They started to take initiative and to influence decisions which were previously beyond their control. During a short phase when experimental conditions were optimal they increased their productivity and earning (20%) to a level which was in fact difficult to handle when the conditions for confirmation of the experimentation was to be bargained between management and union.

This experiment had to be highly controlled from outside the work groups to prevent it from becoming, or being seen as, yet another manipulative technique. However, this high degree of control became in itself a major reason for the experiment to collapse when the workers learned that their shop stewards and the management were not able to utilize the experiences gained as a basis for continuing and improving further the new work system. The research team had failed to establish an adequate system of joint evaluation by management and union on company level to make it part of a strategy of organizational change. Instead, evaluation was made on the national level, by the joint research committee. This evaluation was favourable and resulted in new experiments being started in other companies rather than getting into a tangle with new payment systems and relativities in Christiania Spigerverk. (Further description in Chapter 3.)

2.2. The Hunsfos experiments in papermaking and in chemical pulp

This experiment shows that the basic concept of redesigning work organizations to increase worker's control over their own situation could be applied effectively in process industries with sophisticated technology. On the basis of detailed socio-technical analysis, mainly undertaken by the research team, a change programme was put forward for the pulp department employing about 30 operators. (The company employed 1,000.) The programme was worked out in collaboration with workers and managers from this department. It included improvement of the measurement and information system to be used by the shift teams themselves to control the production process. It involved upgrading of skills, particularly among the workers with low status, and a limited form of job rotation to increase the ability of shift teams to solve problems and handle variations in work load. They would also be able to learn from using the information and control system themselves. The existing plantwide incentive scheme based on production output was to be changed to a departmental bonus system which also took into account quality control.

Information papers were circulated and meetings were held to get involvement on all levels of the firm. But actual commitment to the basic objectives and the specific actions to be taken did not come about until a local action committee was formed to take over the responsibility for the project. Then suggestions for technical improvements started to come forward in great numbers. The operators started to learn from each other and use their new information centre. Some service functions were taken over by the shift groups; quality as well as costs of production started to improve; communication and teamwork between operators improved and attitudes towards the new work system was positive among the majority of workers. A significant minority remained sceptical, mainly those who had previously held privileged jobs and had so far benefited little by the change.

A certain degree of stagnation took place in the second field experiment partly because the new policy to change supervision was not worked out in time – partly because a recession hit the paper industry, forcing management and union to concentrate on problems other than those of the experimental department.

After a period of stagnation the experimental phase was declared over and the new methods of working became standard operating procedure. The company and the union shared the responsibility for the next departmental change project to be started in the paper making department. The paper and pulp experiment had considerable impact on organization policy and vocational training policy on a national level. Diffusion of the new form of work organization within the branch was very limited until 1973. Companies in other industries located in the same region as Hunsfos started their own participation experiments in 1969-70.

The second field experiment benefited from experiences gained in the first. Most important was perhaps the action committee set up by management and union at Hunsfos to transfer the 'ownership' of the project from the outsiders to the people involved in the actual changes taking place. This type of social mechanism has since been used in most Norwegian participation experiments to encourage a self-sustained learning process in changing work organizations. (Further description in Chapter 4.)

2.3. The NOBØ experiment in the metal fabrication industry

This experiment took place in a subsidiary plant with 100 employees in a small community 20 km away from the main plant and the company head-quarters. In the experimental department 30 workers, mostly women, performed semiskilled or unskilled operations producing electric panel heaters. The jobs of metal stamping, drilling, assembly of electrical parts, painting and finishing, could be learned in a few days, or at most weeks, and were organized in typical Tayloristic form. The jobs were narrow and monotonous and pay was based on individual piece rates (MTM standards). This work system was in sharp contrast to the local work – most of the employees came in from housework and farmwork.

The research team was invited by management to start the project at a time when the department had been newly set up and run-in according to 'scientific' management principles. The output was judged by management to be good, the quality and cost figures were satisfactory and the wages good as compared to a similar department in the main plant.

The local shop stewards committee and the superintendent soon grasped the ideas presented by the research team. After a short period of discussion the whole department agreed to start an experiment with semi-autonomous work groups.

All operators were trained to cope with several jobs. 'Contact persons' were chosen to co-ordinate work between groups, while co-ordination between jobs was taken care of by members of work groups. Small technical changes were made to facilitate group work and some service work was decentralised to group level. The wage system was changed from individual piece rates to fixed base rates plus an equally shared departmental bonus on total output within given quality standards. Effective feed back of results was set up in quantitative and qualitative terms. The superintendent moved out of production co-ordination and started to work more on problems between the subsidiary and the main company.

After 10 weeks of controlled experiment the department almost unanimously agreed to continue with the new system and it spread to neighbouring departments with no help from outside. Productivity increased 20% during the experiment and further 10% in the next two years. Quality standards were slightly improved and consistent. Turnover and absenteeism continued to be below average for industry in the area and the time span of responsibility of the workers increased from 2½ hours before the experiment to 2½ months two years later. Ninety per cent of operators were positive about the new system. Significant improvements were experienced in job variation, in participation in decision-making and in collaborative relations in general. Only a small improvement was seen in learning on the job since the work itself was much the same. The real learning was in managing themselves for up to 2½ months at a stretch.

There was very limited diffusion of the new ideas on work organization from the experimental site to the main company. No basic change was seen in management philosophy above plant level. However, when a new and larger plant was built to take over the production from the experimental one, the group system was introduced and is still practiced among the 400 workers without any supervisors. The trade union was significantly strengthened at the plant level, but the experiment was not actively supported by regional and national union leaders, and did not lead to policy changes on these levels. However, the NOBØ case became some sort of model for shop floor democracy promoted by the unions. And it did strengthen opposition to Tayloristic work organization and related incentive systems. The experimental plant was visited by the media, a great number of study teams from other parts of the country and from abroad, particularly from Sweden. Those who had been directly involved in the experiment were somewhat concerned over this great publicity as no basic changes seemed to have occurred in the management philosophy of the firm or in the policy of the national union. (Further description in Chapter 5.)

2.4. The Norsk Hydro fertilizer experiment

This experiment was undertaken by a large chemical manufacturing firm in collaboration with the chemical workers union and the research group. One operating fertilizer plant with about 100 employees and a new one under construction were chosen as field sites. Rather poor labour-management relations had developed in the firm over the years, characterised by highly bureaucratized organizational structures and tight control systems on the one hand and restrictive practices among organized labour on the other. A new president of the company and a newly elected chief shop steward decided that something had to be done about this, particularly as the firm was faced with severe market conditions while production costs were rising rapidly. The long term changes in the labour market with a more highly educated labour force would also require changes toward a more challenging work situation at shop floor level.

The most significant aspect of the experiment was the shift in basic principles of organizational design which took place while the new plant was put into operation. The original design had just been presented and recruitment was about to start when the action committee took over and started to modify the plans. Semi-autonomous shift groups were established instead of specialized, individualized work roles. All operators were given a basic course in process technology and all workers were granted the right to learn wider areas of plant operation either through practice or by special courses. Levels of payment were determined by the number of plant areas workers were qualified to operate. A plant bonus was established to stimulate learning on plant level to operate within quality limits, to avoid wastage and pollution etc. Previously they had been payed for the job they were performing at the moment according to a detailed job classification system. Instead of increasing the number of assistant foremen (charge hands) from 4 in the old plant to 12 in the new one, this position was dropped completely. The work groups were going to handle their own internal co-ordination. The simpler maintenance work was to be integrated into the shift teams and the number of skilled craftsmen in the new plant went down from 12 in the original plan to 8. A team of 12 day shift workers and a foreman, who according to the plan should have taken care of transportation cleaning etc., were never employed, since their work was done by the shift groups. It was agreed that no worker should be employed in such dead end jobs. The number of men in the shift groups remained on the level set out in the original plan, but the average of 12 varied from team to team over time.

Specialist and service departments were decentralized to encourage autonomy on individual, group and plant level. For some functions, like training, quality control and rationalization this did occur, while other service functions remained centralized. This caused some stagnation problems at a later stage. A new philosophy of management was initiated, emphasizing participation in decision-making on all levels. This philosophy was not worked through effectively and diffusion of the new ideas of work organization was slow.

During the autumn of 1967 when the new plant was gradually put into operation and the last group of operators were to be recruited and trained, the old fertilizer plant started to reorganize. The immediate reason was that a productivity agreement had been signed, covering all Norsk Hydro workers. A significant increase in wages would be gained if reduced manning was achieved by transfer to vacancies in plants needing new workers. The workers of the old fertilizer plant would have liked to enter the agreement but rejected the new manning scheme worked out by consultants working in other plants. Instead the action committee of the experimental plant was asked to carry out the analysis of manning needs. From this point on the old fertilizer plant followed the new one in organizational design.

When the new plant had been in operation for two months the action committee reported on progress and a joint meeting of management and union representatives advised the firm to start similar projects in several other plants. This led to some successful and several unsuccessful attempts to introduce the new organizational policy in the corporation as a whole. For further discussion of this development the reader should turn to Chapter 6.

The first four field experiments are presented in the following four chapters. They will give the reader a detailed account of what was done and how the changes took place in different companies, with different technologies and in different social settings. (Those who are not interested in these details may turn to Chapter 7.)

3. The Wire Drawing Mill

3.1. Selection of the Wire Drawing Department of Christiana Spigerverk as the experimental site

The Christiana Spigerverk was one of the metal working firms selected by the Joint Committee (of LO and NAF for research into industrial democracy) as suitably representative for purposes of experimentally demonstrating ways of achieving at the workplace the conditions of interest, initiative and creativity required for the growth of effective industrial democracy.

The company was part of a growing enterprise of national standing, and experiments here were likely to have some potential impact upon the iron metal manufacturing branch, one of the important sectors of the Norwegian economy. The company had some 1200 workers in its Oslo plants and a long tradition of orderly labour-management relations and of advanced welfare programmes. It maintains close contact with the leaders of Trade Union Council and the Confederation of Employers. The plant is situated in an area with a long tradition in the industry. It was here, along a river in the Oslo Valley, that the textile and iron manufacturing industries started to grow more than a hundred years ago. The management of the company was in the process of change. The older generation of managers had recently withdrawn, after having rebuilt the firm from near bankruptcy, when it was taken over by a young engineer in the 1920s. A new generation of professional managers took over in the early sixties. The company had gradually developed into a vertically integrated corporation with a very strong position in some fields of production on the national market and good international contacts on the technological and raw materials side. Marketing had not been troubled by major fluctuations although foreign, and to some degree national, competition became keener at the time the experiment started.

Following three months of intermittent contact, it was unanimously agreed by management, union and the researchers, at meetings on 17 January 1964, that the first steps towards experimentation should be taken and that the best place for this was the Wire Drawing Department.

The commitment of management and union was limited at this stage, at the specific request of the researchers, to carrying out a socio-technical analysis of the Wire Drawing Department. No questions of further commitment was involved. If and when the researchers, as a result of their studies, presented recommendations for experimentation, the union and management would consider what further commitments, if any, they could enter into.

The selection of the Wire Drawing Department appeared to have been governed by several considerations. Other departments were involved in wage changes that might prove too unsettled for experiments involving job design. The economics of the Wire Drawing Department were considered to be less sensitive than that of the other departments to the envisaged experiments and the relative independence of the Department would help to limit the effects of any unpredicted disturbance that might occur. Furthermore, it was felt that the Department had a good deal to gain if the experiments should prove in any way successful.

The high turnover and low morale indicated that there was plenty of room for improvement. From the viewpoint of the researchers, this was a particularly attractive place to start because the jobs had many of the features common to light engineering – one man/one machine, strictly limited and routine task field, little or no interdependence, and individual incentives.

3.2. Characteristics of the wire drawing job

Field work for the socio-technical analysis commenced in February and the recommendations arising therefrom were presented to management and unions at meetings on 11 June 1964.

The details of this analysis are presented elsewhere. (Marek,[1] 1964) For the purposes of this report we will summarily present those features of the wire drawing job that influenced the research proposals for the new job design. These are:

1. *The layout* is characterized by some twenty wire-drawing benches, 10-12 meters long, placed across a rather dirty and noisy room. Raw material in the form of large bundles of thick wire is brought in by the fork lift truck operator from the adjoining room where it has been treated in chemical

1. See Report 1. Industrial Democracy Project; Wire Mill of the Christiania Spigerverk. By Julius Marek, Knut Lange, Per Engelstad, Institute for Industrial Social Research, NTH, Trondheim, June 1964.

baths. After being run across the benches for reduction in thickness the wire is taken off and bundled at the output end of the bench, to be taken away by truck for weighing and storing.
2. The main tasks of the operator are to weld bundles of wire together at the input end of the bench, fit the wire onto the bench around a number of revolving blocks, through the reducing dies and to the bundling arrangement at the output end. Apart from the welding machine he uses heavy tongs and other hand tools to do this and electric motors to pull the wire across the benches.

3. A profile of the activity level throughout a typical shift looks like the following:

For a considerable part of his time the wire drawer is inactive. During this time there is little to occupy him or interest him. This is interspersed with routine tasks of welding together the batches of wire that come to the machine for further reduction in thickness, and taking off and binding the coils of finished wire. Much more demanding are the unpredictable breakages that occur in the wire. When these happen he must respond promptly by shutting off the motors that are pulling the wire at high speed through the reducing dies. Failure to act quickly might produce new breakages. Having stopped the motors, he must then cut away the tangled wire, force the ends through the dies, weld them together and get the wire running smoothly again. This work not only arises unpredictably and suddenly but must also be carried out in the face of varying technical difficulties and strong pressures to be as quick as possible. Although the individual breakage is unpredictable, the probability of their occurrence varies with, for instance, the quality of the wire, which lies outside operator control. As a result there can be considerable variations from the above profile which we have presented as typical. The variation is not so much in the routine tasks (except insofar as they are lessened if the wire is not running through well) but between the proportion of 'slack time' and rushed time, between an easy and a difficult shift.

4. There is no interdependence between workers. Each man has his own bench to which he comes on every shift. (For special technical reasons two particular benches may be run by one man.) He is paid for the production or the down-time on his own machine alone (at standard rates, but the down-time is to be recorded by the worker himself and hence subject to negotiation with the foreman). If a neighbouring bench is running into a great deal of difficulty with wire breakages, the worker is expected to ignore

it and concern himself only with his own bench even though he may have nothing to do. If so directed by the foreman he may stop the bench and give a hand with a heavy lift, but, otherwise mutual help does not occur. The most frequent social interactions are the relatively infrequent ones with a maintenance man, foreman or the tool room (for new dies). Changes in dies occurred on the average only once in four shifts so this contact is almost irrelevant. From interviews with 38 men it appeared that 28 had one or two contacts per shift with the foreman, six more and one less contact. Voluntary interactions are usually few in number. Typically the operator spends his slack time on a seat partly hidden from sight between his bench and the back of the neighbouring bench.

Table III. 1. Observed contacts per hour.

			With others (excluding foreman)		With foreman	
	Within Group A	Within Group B	Group A	Group B	Group A	Group B
During experiment	1.3	4.1	0.7	0.7	0.4	0.1
Traditional conditions	0.3	0.7	0.9	2.7	0.1	0.4

All social contacts per hour	Group A	Group B
During experiment	2.4	4.9
Traditional conditions	1.3	3.8

This low level of social interaction seems to be of particular relevance when one considers that for many people the co-operation of others would make stressful situations like handling wire breakages both more tolerable

Graph III.1. Activity profiles on one operator for one shift.

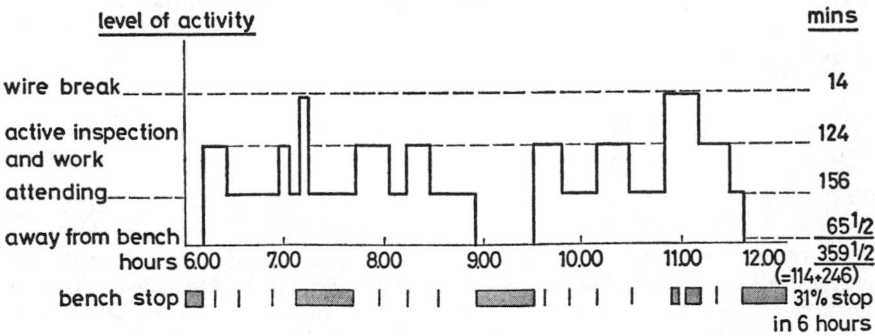

Bench 10 Sat. 9/1/60
(V=1815 m/m; Dim 2.08 bl. st.; 100 kg Rings; 3 band; 6 dies)

and more manageable. There is also danger in wire drawing. The support of others is a known help in coping with dangerous situations, but we were unable to determine the significance of this for the wire drawers.

One other feature of the situation acts to strengthen the individualism of the Wire Drawing Department. There is greater variation between productivity of benches than between the men who operate them on different shifts, so that men who have the good benches jealously guard the personal advantage this gives and tend to be hostile to any suggestion of sharing it. This is by no means the whole of the picture. There were other ways in which individuals could advance their personal interests. A continuous revision of piece rates takes place, through the way that the single workers go to the foreman or department head and claim revised time studies. Clever negotiators and eager complainers may obtain better piecerates than others. This way there is established a situation where there may be grounds for saying that many other criteria than productivity determine earnings and earning differentials.

5. The prevailing attitudes and feeling of the workers reflect the objective characteristics of the situation. On the one hand they find the work to be boring, lacking variety and lacking in attraction; on the other hand, owing

Table III.2. Attitudes towards aspects of the wire drawing job.[2]

Very interesting	3	Very varied	1	Great deal to do	1
Interesting	3	Varied	4	Much to do	1
Neither	17	Neither	4	Neither	24
Boring	13	Monotonous	16	Little to do	8
Very boring	4	Very monotonous	15	Very little to do	6
Very relaxing	8				
Relaxing	9				
Neither	4				
Tense	13				
Very tense	5				

2. From interviews with 40 wire workers; 31 working in the main hall, 8 from the thin wire hall and one from the bolt wire benches. The interviews showed that most of the men found working conditions unpleasantly hot in summer, dirty, dusty and noisy and did not like the shift work. They were divided on opinions about the safety aspect of the work. These conditions were not changed by the experiment and hence these data are not considered in this report.

presumably to the threat of breakage, some workers found the situation produced tension. The following comments were typical:

a. 'First, I would say it was a dead dull job, standing there day after day.'
b. 'Monotonous. It is the same over and over again when you stand by the same machine.'
c. 'Not much to tell about. Dull work. Not work for me. A dead work, not interesting, the same every day.'

On the other hand, the men generally favoured the way the job was organized. Questioned about being 'master of their own bench' all but one man (out of 28 asked this question) regarded this as a positive feature. Questioned further about whether they would like to do this work together with a group or in pairs the men answered as follows:

Table III.3. Attitude towards working together in groups or in pairs. (N = 38)

Positive	2
Conditionally positive	12
Neutral	2
Negative	22

In other words the individualistic organisation of the job was strongly supported by the belief that this is the way it should be. These attitudes could have arisen because of a process of selection such that sociable men would not stay long on this lonely job and that the men staying on would be those who prefer loneliness. However, we doubt that this is the full explanation. At least as big a part seemed to be played by mutual mistrust and misperceptions. The twelve who gave qualified support to the idea of co-operative work did so only on the condition that they could choose their work mates. Others who rejected the idea spontaneously went on to explain that this was not because they disliked working this way but because they did not think one could find others in the Department able and willing to work properly in a team. In line with this interpretation is the fact that so many of the men refer to the loneliness – the lack of social contact – as a bad feature of the job. It would seem, on balance, that while some individuals may have found a positive value in the lack of interaction on the job, the majority regret it but put up with it because they do not in any case expect to find other industrial jobs that are, all told, much better. That these attitudes were not only stably rooted in objective job characteristics but also strongly held to be 'correct attitudes' may be inferred from the length of experience of the men with these jobs.

Table III. 4. Length of employment in the wire mill.

6 months or less	6 months – 2 years	3-7 years	8-16 years	20 years or more
2	6	13	15	4

3.3. Recommendations

From a detailed analysis of the technical operations and of the various kinds of work loads created by the process (including requirements for monitoring), it became obvious that (a) without a technical solution to the problem of breakages it would not be possible to redesign the job so that, although done on an individual basis, it would have a suitable activity profile (as judged by the criteria presented earlier), and (b) it was not possible to see how any solution in terms of an individually based job could overcome the lack of optimal social interaction.

From the same data it was, however, possible to calculate that the work loads generated by different sets of benches could yield better activity profiles if the men were free to go to the work wherever it occurred and were not compelled to wait at one bench till the work came to them. This solution entailed that a group of men would take responsibility for a set of benches and each man would work at whatever was required at the time, regardless of which bench was involved. It seemed reasonably certain from the evidence that this method of working could cope with the problems of monitoring and with the peaks of work that could be expected from simultaneous wire breakages on more than one bench in the set.[3] This solution automatically solved also the problem of inadequate social interaction.

After the analytical exercises had established the technical feasibility of the group method (in terms of past records) it was necessary to formulate

3. On the past records of the benches considered most suitable for testing the method of group working it appeared that the probability at any one time of one in six benches being stopped for breakage was approximately one in three, one in eleven of two and less than one in fifty of three. In the unlikely event of three simultaneous breakages, it seemed better to shut down one machine for the time rather than build a labour reserve adequate to cope with it.

the conditions that were necessary or desirable for experimentally testing the method in the conditions prevailing in the Wire Drawing Department. The general recommendation – its rationale and the statement of conditions – were communicated at the management and union meetings of 11 June 1964. The 'statement of conditions' was as follows:

The requirements for experimentally testing group methods of working in the Wire Drawing Department.

1. *Size of group.* Not less than four and preferably more – *with more machines than men.* Otherwise it is difficult to see how they would make effective use of the time saved and it was considered that it would be difficult to break the old system of one man, one machine.
2. *Wages.* For the period of the experiment it was felt essential that (i) the men participating should have a guaranteed minimum so that they would not lose financially from their participation; (ii) they should have a financial incentive for trying to develop optimum methods of working as a group.
3. *Membership.* The recruitment to the experiment to be entirely voluntary. In the absence of any tradition of co-operative working in wire drawing, it was considered to be essential that the members of the experiment both wished to participate and were accepted by the other members as reliable co-operators.
4. *Method of work.* The minimum requirement was a separation off of the welding task at the input end. Beyond this it was considered that the most appropriate arrangement was one in which the men spread themselves across the input end and had overlapping fields of responsibility. However, it was felt that the groups should be left to find their own specific method of working.
5. *Agreement on the status and duration of the experiment.* It was considered essential that both parties accept that this was simply an experiment and involved neither party, even in discussing its findings if they did not wish to do this. The experiment was to provide a basis in experience for the subsequent discussion of change; it was not the thin end of the wedge of change. Three months was thought long enough to see whether the group system of working was worthy of further serious consideration by the parties concerned. It was recommended that the experiment should automatically cease and the members revert to normal working unless there was

a new and explicit agreement by both parties to continue.

6. *Limits of group responsibility.* It was necessary that any experimental group operate within the usual restraints to maintain safety and to protect company property from misuse or damage. Production would likewise need to be within reasonable expectations for the men and equipment involved.

Beyond these requirements it was thought that there were conditions that were desirable although not essential at the beginning:

1. That the layout and control of equipment be modified to facilitate group working. The existing layout placed a premium on individual working, as movement between benches could take place easily only at the output end, and controls for each bench were located on that bench. If the full system of group working was to emerge, then the operators would need to be able to monitor several benches at a time, to be able to stop them with distant controls and to have a quick and easy path from one machine to another from either end. In the absence of this there would be either excessive running around or some degree of the one man, one machine system would be entailed.
2. That some of the simpler maintenance tasks should devolve upon the group or that some type of maintenance man should be attached.
3. That trainees should be introduced into the groups.
4. That the group be provided with knowledge of its results (and of planning). Under the old system the individual could be expected to have a fair idea of the progress of work throughout the shift for his own bench. With a group moving about and sharing responsibility it would be more difficult for the members to judge how they were progressing and hence to adjust their pace, unless special steps were taken to measure group performance.

3.4. Realisation of the requirements for experimentally testing the group method of working

The preceding section outlines what was felt to be theoretically necessary and desirable. It was obviously undesirable to set up an experiment in complete isolation of the labour agreements holding for other parts of the company and hence the management and union had to negotiate the conditions that could be actually set up. They had also to take the steps to achieve what they agreed upon.

The initiation of the project on the shop floor was far from easy although we had the backing of the union as well as of top management. The men were indifferent as to the importance attached to the project by their national leaders. We found that information on the political aspects of industrial democracy from the Trade Union was left unread in the locker rooms. And the men could not see that other aspects of industrial democracy could bring them any immediate gains in terms of better working conditions. The appeal from shop stewards got them to agree to co-operate in the project, but the research team was quite aware after the first formal meeting with the work crews that very little information had come across and no commitment, except possibly of a negative character, had emerged.[4] Attitudes on the shop floor were still very much the same as emerged in the very first meeting. On that occasion the temper of the meeting was extremely cool – some fifty men facing the project leader struggling to explain what it was all about; most of the workers looking at the floor or past him out of the window. The shop steward committee, sitting with the speaker and the rest of the research group in the back of the room felt equally uneasy. Only one serious question was put to the speaker who had been introduced pleasantly by the chief shop steward. A little man, known for his sharp tongue, and his ability to voice the negative opinions of his workmates, asked: 'Is it true, what I have heard, that you are the new 'axe committee' who is helping to rationalize more of us out of our jobs?' The explanations of the shop stewards and the researchers over the subsequent months did little to dispel these fears. We had, however, no choice other than to proceed and to hope that the backing we had outside the department and our face-to-face contacts on the shop floor would gradually change the situation.

As a result of this, the experiment started on Monday 7 September under the following basic conditions:

1. *Size of group.* The union insisted that the seven benches chosen for the experiment – 9, 10, 11, 12, 13, 14 and 15 – should be manned by the same number of men as required under the present system, i.e. six men (benches 14 and 15, on very thin wire, were usually run by one man).
2. *Wages.* Both parties agreed to a guaranteed minimum wage which was approximately one per cent above the average earnings for the preceding four weeks. It was agreed that the group would receive extra incentive payment for production over and above the average for these benches for the preceding four weeks. It was assumed that this could be calculated in

4. Our first experience, but not our last, of a 'negative Hawthorne effect'.

the same way as the existing price rates, except for calculation of down-time. Down-time was to be determined from the automatic datalogger, attached to each bench and not subject to the customary modification by the foreman.

3. *Membership*. It was left to the shop stewards to find volunteers for the experiment. There was a strong tradition of each man being attached to one machine and those with good machines were naturally very attached to them. To minimise disturbance in this setting, the shop stewards did their best to get the men already on the chosen benches (9-15 inclusive) to agree to participate in the experiment. All agreed except one man on the B-shift. He was moved to another bench. It was already clear in the week before the experiment started that these men did not see themselves as volunteers in the ordinary sense of the word. They were in the experiment mainly because they did not wish to leave their benches and were not strongly against participating. At least one man in the B group (afternoon shift) felt that he had been forced into participating. In no way had the men selected each other as co-operators.
4. *Working methods*. Management and union agreed that for the purpose of the experiment the workers should try to share out the work on a group basis along the lines suggested by the research team. The participating workers themselves agreed to have two people constantly on welding at the input end, but were otherwise unwilling to go much beyond rotation from bench to bench and to the welding job, and to some degree of mutual help particularly during breakages.
5. *Status and duration of the experiment*. Management and union both accepted the definition of the status and recommendation for the duration of the experiment put forward by the researchers. Communication to the workers in the mill was not so successful particularly in the case of the majority who had not been personally approached as potential participants. Amongst them there were feelings that the experiment already implied management's commitment to change along these lines.

Regarding those conditions which were seen as desirable but not necessary at the beginning of the experiment, the position was as follows:

1. *Layout and control equipment*. It was not considered feasible to change the layout just for this experiment. The need for a stop button near the welding position was recognised. Only two could be put in before the start owing to shortage of maintenance staff. All stop buttons were ready after a fortnight.

2. *Maintenance*. One of the maintenance men was assigned to giving special attention to the experimental group's requests. In addition, a special tool kit was given to the representative of each group.
3. *Trainees*. This question was left open at the beginning and only later were trainees attached.
4. *Knowledge of results*. To begin with, one of the research team took measures of group production twice per shift and entered these, plus estimated earnings, on a wall chart opposite the experimental benches. On this chart there was marked also the average production and earnings for the preceding ten weeks of non-experimental working and the base line of production equivalent to the guaranteed earnings. Later this task was taken over by a clerk, who gave the production and earnings of the preceding day each morning around 11 a.m.

3.5. Analysis of the experimental experiences

The experience of the groups needs to be examined separately for the three phases. During the first phase of four weeks, the three basic conditions (optimal manning, incentive earnings and voluntary membership) did *not* exist for either group A or group B. On the Wednesday of the fourth week the men met and decided that the original groups should be disbanded and the experiment continued with one group of real volunteers. The question of incentive earnings was renegotiated with management during the rest of that week.

Phase two lasted for only the fifth and sixth weeks. During this phase one of the volunteers was absent and the group took advantage of the situation to run the extra machine and thus achieved for the first and only time the conditions of optimal manning.

Phase three lasted for the remaining seven weeks of the experiment. A second group of volunteers started up in the afternoon shift and ran for the last five weeks. Throughout phase three, the groups were voluntary and the wage agreement negotiated at the end of phase one was still in force. However, both groups were now under strong pressure not to run extra benches, not to engage in what would be seen by the other wire workers as rate busting and they were restrained by union and management from realising their potential in reduction of working hours.

The following table summarises the differences between phases:

Table III. 5. Main phase of the experiment: realisation, non-realisation of conditions*.

Phase	Week	Group A (A') conditions 1 (manning)	2 (wages)	3 (voluntary membership)	Group B (B') conditions 1	2	3
I	1	–	–	–	–	–	–
	2	–	–	–	–	–	–
	3	–	–	–	–	–	–
	4	–	–	–	–	–	–
II	5	x	–	x			
	6	x	(x)	x			
III	7	–	(x)	x			
	8	–	(x)	x			
	9	–	(x)	x			
	10	–	(x)	x	–	(x)	x
	11	–	(x)	x	–	(x)	x
	12	–	(x)	x	–	(x)	x
	13	–	(x)	x	–	(x)	x

* Condition fulfilled: x; condition partly fulfilled: (x); condition unfilfilled: –.

3.5.1. Phase I

1. *Manning.* Almost without exception both groups stuck to their original decision of not running at less than one man per machine (allowing for the fact that benches 14 and 15 were customarily run by one man). The exception was during the third week. On Wednesday 23 September one of the researchers suggested to B group members that they try to run bench 13 which was idle because one of the group was absent. This suggestion was taken up and the bench ran for about half an hour till a replacement arrived. The following day, on the initiative of one group member, the bench, again empty, was pulled along for several hours. When this became known to A group they strongly condemned this as a breach of their agreement to uphold the rule of one man, one machine.

2. *Wages.* Already from the first day it became apparent to the researchers that there was something basically wrong with calculating group earnings on the old individual piece rates, and downtimes by means of readings off the 'data-logger' or by means of the downtime claimed by the workers in their downtime labels. As the graph of production went up, the graph of estimated earnings was either unresponsive or even declined. Information about

this was given to management and the chief shop steward who made representations to management. He wanted to use this incident to claim a general revision of the payment system on the wire mill. Also it became quite evident that the 'agreement' between the parties about the experiment was very vague and was conceived differently by the parties on such a major theme as the guarantee time. A new method of calculation was introduced by management in the third week and the whole question was renegotiated at the end of the fourth week. A broader worry about earnings had already appeared in the second week. At a meeting of the two groups, one man from B complained that there was some pressure in his group to compete with group A and 'this was wrong as it pressed piece rates'. He received some support for his views. This suggests that there was still some doubt about the status of the experiment.

3. *Voluntary participation.* As already mentioned, before the experiment had even begun, one man in B group had been vociferous about being compelled to participate. At the meeting on Monday 14 September, one other member of B group and one of A group said they wanted to withdraw. The absence of mutual selection was reflected in a statement to the meeting by an A group man 'that you couldn't find six men here who are really willing to work together – co-operation doesn't work here'.

4. *Methods of work.* Throughout this phase, there was considerable conservatism and lack of initiative. Two major factors seemed to operate here. On the one hand, the researchers felt that it was essential for the men to be free to exercise their initiative from the beginning and hence develop a group method of working that they would see as their own. Past experience with autonomous work groups suggested that there is not one best way for all groups of men even for the same technological systems. The researchers therefore concentrated on creating the conditions where the men would feel attracted and impelled towards learning new ways. On the other hand, the existing work culture was very strongly tied to the marriage of one man to one machine. As shown earlier, most of the men had years of experience in this system (often with the same machine). One of the benches was burdened with unusually bad wire during the first and second weeks. This tied an operator to this bench most of the time and reduced the freedom to experiment and increased the general anxiety of the groups. (The start of Phase II was blessed by good wire rod so that the operators got time to try out new ways of organising their work.)

The high turnover of trainees and new workers in the mill (six out of ten quit within the first eighteen months of employment) suggests that not only had most of these men become habituated to this work, but they had been selected out by the system as the ones least put off by the isolation of the job and its peculiar rhythm of indolence and exasperating wire trouble. These men believed that they knew their machines in a way that even the foremen did not. They could not conceive that the machines could be run economically in any other way. Even those men who strove very hard to get their teams to make a go of the experiment confessed that:

'In the beginning I regarded the experiment as a hopeless case. This was because we could not see the work distribution, but now we have worked such a long time together that we know each other and work together.'

'The reason why I was sceptical regarding the group probably was that you were so very sure this was going to work out, and I felt you had no practical experience and I was very doubtful as to whether you had any basis for what you were saying. This was maybe the major reason why I reacted like I did, but another thing was that I actually regarded it as hopeless to find a group that was actually willing to go together.'

'We have talked about making some suggestions. I am sure it would pay off if we could only get started so that we could use the possibilities (of group work). But we haven't done that. Rather we have kept back a little.'

'I had no real belief in this from the beginning. But now I think it will work as soon as we have become more accustomed to it.'

Failure to achieve optimal manning, wage incentive and the absence of voluntary participation reduced the pressure on the men to develop methods of group working. The fact that the men had not chosen each other as team mates lessened the possibility that they could sink their individual interests in the group interest.

This conservatism was shown in both groups. They both accepted the minimum specifications of separating out the task of welding at the input end as a special job and of taking turns at this. In itself this placed a strain on the tradition of one man, one machine, as the men remaining on the benches had to take some responsibility for monitoring neighbouring benches and there was some inducement to help with bundling the output wire or even with wire breakages. 'If there is hard running you can get help in different ways to get or keep the bench going. They can bundle, weld or do something like that while you concentrate on the break.' It also modified the work profile. While on the welding job the work was fairly constant. The remaining bench jobs were simplified by the exclusion of the input welding but the monitoring task demanded more, as several benches usually had to be watched. 'With someone welding the coils (at the input end) the others can be closer to each other and help each other.' Because of the physical layout, it was less easy to monitor from the old position of a comfortable seat between the machines. Beyond this a basic difference appeared between groups A and B. Group A decided on a rotation that ran from benches 15 to 9 to welding and back to bench 15. In this way, the very considerable variation between work load on the different machines was ironed out. 'The work becomes more varied, and you are not so tied to one machine. You get more function into the whole work. It is absolutely an advantage for the machines where the running is hard, and where the dimensions vary.' 'Yes, I think the job is more varied, that is very important. And then work is more evenly distributed on all workers, because there are some hard benches, and some light ones.'

Group B was troubled by absenteeism all the four weeks it existed. In this group some of the men insisted on sticking to the bench they had before the experiment, although they took their turn at welding and kept an eye on their neighbour's bench if he was doing his turn at welding. Thus in this group there was still the old business of some men continually carrying more of a load than others but with the added disincentive that they only got an equal share of the group earnings. In the first week there was already an angry outburst from one man who felt he was being unfairly burdened under this system. Both groups ran into the difficulty that owing to the old system not all had had experience of welding certain classes of wire (which only went to some of the machines). Group A's rotation system created the other difficulty that the men had to learn to operate benches other than their own.

5. *Satisfaction.* The change from Phase I occurred before the systematic survey of attitudes that had been planned for mid-point of the experiment. As a result, attitudes in this phase can only be judged from the records of day-to-day contacts with the workers and observational records of the meetings. As we have already noted, there was little cause for satisfaction with earnings and plenty of evidence of dissatisfaction with them coming to a head in the meetings at the end of the fourth week. Similarly there were in each group men who were dissatisfied with their inclusion in the group or dissatisfied with some of the others for their unco-operative attitude.

Already in the second week, the local shop stewards became worried because of uncertainty and lack of enthusiasm in the work groups. They called a meeting of all the group members and the chairman of the union was present. Several complaints over technical difficulties and lack of co-operation were voiced. Those who were positive explained how they had strived to keep control over the situation. One of them raised the question whether it might be possible to try to run the machines during the lunch break so that the men could get some encouragement. He was told to wait and see. Group members felt uneasy because the other workers in the wire drawing mill did not seem to know much about the experiment. Although informed, they were sceptical towards the group system. Group members found it difficult to answer questions and explain potential advantages of the group system of working. The importance of the experiment in developing more democratic work relations on the shop floor seemed not to impress the majority of workers. However, they were deeply concerned about protecting the present piece rate earnings.

'One thing must be very clear before one can start to co-operate (like this) . . . There must be a firm contract with management so that this does not hit back at us. There is anxiety among us. . . not in our group, but among the others. . . I believe people might have expected a larger advantage than we have achieved so far. That could come later. . .'
'We had to listen to a lot of bad talk – those of us who had started up.'

The development of attitudes during Phase I is illustrated by the following table. The evidence for the first and third weeks comes from interviews at the benches, and for the second and fourth weeks from meetings at which the groups discussed their experience and decided upon a future course of action. (Table III.6 next page.)

Several facts emerge from this table. Most of the group members started off being sceptical or unwilling. Those who (in spite of scepticism) tried to make the best of it developed a positive attitude, those who were unwilling to try remained negative. The exceptions are interesting, but of secondary interest.

In Group A, the prevailing attitude was positive, while in Group B the positive ones were unable to pull the negative ones along. Group A had from the beginning two members (5 and 6a) who were unwilling to try the possibilities of group work. One of them (6a) left the group after two weeks and a substitute was put in by the foreman. This new man was initially unwilling, but changed his mind and seemed to accept group work. The other negative member of Group A (5) referred to 'lack of co-operation' among men in the wire drawing room. Still he volunteered to go on at the end of Phase I, but now he was not accepted by the others.

In Group B the predominant attitude was negative, even though this

Table III. 6. Attitudes to the group system.

	At the start	During week 37	During week 38	During week 39	During week 40	Volunteers for Phase II (voting)
GROUP A						
Member						
1	Sceptical	+	+?	+	+	+
2	Co-operation impossible	+	− (no co-operation)	−	0	+
3	Sceptical	+	+	+	+	+
4	Sceptical	+	+	0	0	−
5	Sceptical	−	− (no enthusiasm)	− (quit the group)	−	−
6a	−	−	−			
6b				− (selected by foreman)	+	+
GROUP B						
1	+	+	+ (no co-operation)	+	+	+
2	+	+	−	Ill	Ill	Ill
3	−	−	−	−	−	−
4	−	−	−	−	−	−
5	+	+ (notice of leaving)	+	− (no co-operation)	−	−
6	+	Ill	Ill	+	+	+

+ = positive attidude; − = negative attitude; 0 — neutral attidude; ? — unknown attitude.

group had a small majority of positive members from the beginning. The absence of one man who was sick caused difficulties in arranging good work organisation, and the flow of production. The group representative of Group B did not initiate his group into new ways of working as much as Group A did, and he was not as eager to pull his men along. (He had actually applied for a new job outside the company before group work was introduced and he gave notice of leaving in the middle of Phase I.) The result was that those initially positive lost interest in group work. On top of this, one more man turned sick and the group was never complete during Phase I. (One bench in the middle of the work area was left idle or was run by a reserve member of the group.) The negative attitude of Group B was strengthened by a special incident. One of the old wire drawers had refused to join the experimental group and had been moved from his old bench. This made one of the group membeis 'feel like a Judas' because he had joined.

A problem for a majority of group members was the feeling of making fools of themselves coming on to new benches which they did not know.

The local shop steward of the wire drawing room was a member of Group B but was not its formal representative. He tried his best to create some team spirit by encouraging competition between the two groups. He was condemned by his work mates for doing something which might look like rate busting. He was also the one who responded to a suggestion of one of the researchers and tried running an extra machine. For this he was condemned by a member of Group A for 'breaking the agreement'.

Where satisfaction with the new method was expressed, it was with:
a. the improved profile of shift activity;
b. the increased contact with others;
c. 'time went faster.'

6. *Production.* For this short period, the only reasonable performance indicator was that of productivity. As is typical of mixed men-machine systems this was not an easy thing to measure. On the measure selected, we find that despite the novelty of the working methods, production fell very little below achieved by traditional methods. There was a general recognition that very little more production could be extracted from the technical system without either changing the traditional manning ratio, or

Graph III.2. Productivity of experimental benches. Moving average of 3 shifts.

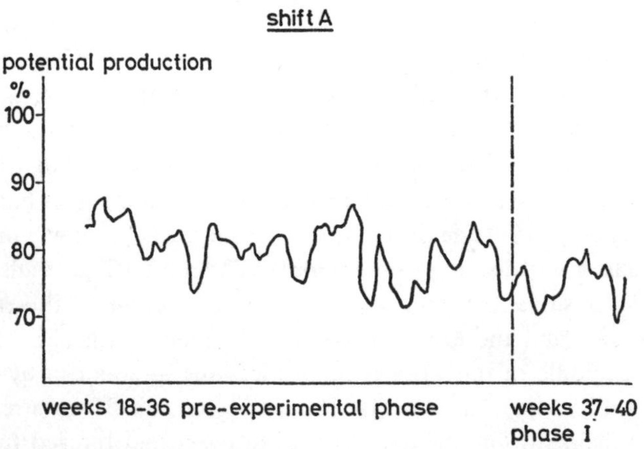

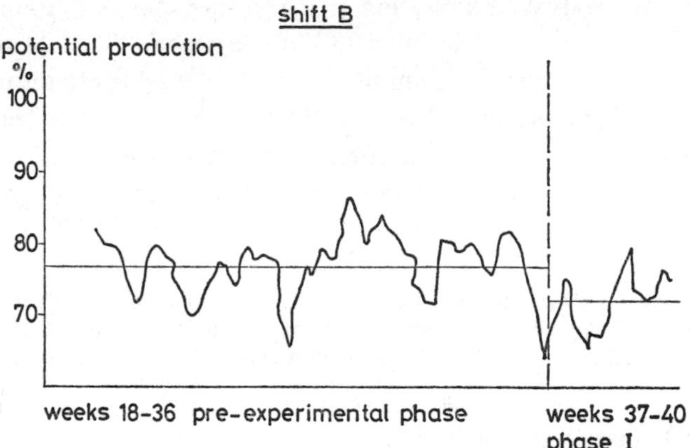

using the time now available to run the machines during meal breaks (while workers took the break in turn).

With experimental conditions far from being optimal, as indicated above, one must be careful when interpreting these production results. The most striking thing is that production did not fall much more below the pre-experimental level. If these groups had really changed their work organisation radically, a much clearer drop in productivity could have occurred before the advantage of new methods of work could follow a period of relearning.

Group B showed fairly clearly that greater use of the old method could produce as much as the group method even though it did not allow for as much interpersonal interaction or improvement of the profile of work activity.

3.5.2. Phase II

This phase was characterised by the reconstitution of *one* new group on the basis of real volunteers and a re-negotiated earnings incentive. It had the other critical characteristic that the sickness of one member made it possible for the group to take over an extra machine. For some reason they decided to do this although in Phase I much the same people had condenmed a man in Group B for trying to do so.

Production during the two weeks of the phase was well above the average for this number of men (but not above what they could have done with an extra man on the same number of benches). Individual interviews in the week after Phase II showed that all the members of this volunteer group were satisfied with the system as then running. Some dissatisfaction still existed with the wages. At a meeting on 7 October, the new group indicated that the incentive was still insufficient. In the second week of this phase, there was a spontaneous move amongst the other workers to set up another group on the afternoon shift. However, the success of the volunteer group in these two weeks gave particular force to some of the argument aroused before the experiment started. As two leading members of the group saw it (in their own words):

'During the weeks we were running all the machines with one man short people from the outside interferred. We felt all right because we were managing . . . There was a hullabaloo when they saw that we were pulling along an extra bench. But we did pull it along.'

One of the earliest opponents stated:

'It was a terrible thing. Group A act against all of our previous agreements; they produce much more and take on much more. Furthermore, it is impossible if someone is threatened with dismissal if he does not do what he is told (meaning in this only if he does join a group there).

1. *Attitudes toward the group system of work organisation.* As we have indicated above it was in fact only during this second phase of the experiment that the group system had a fair chance of proving its merits. At least three of the necessary conditions for change did exist, although some desirable conditions were still lacking. The *manning*, with four men on five machines, gave room for some extra initiative to be released on group basis. The members would not as easily slip back into the old one man, one-machine system. The *earnings* calculated on a new basis gave some real incentive. The members of the group had chosen *voluntarily* to join and to work with each other. Statements from each of the participants working under these conditions constitute significant evidence. Comparing the new and the old system of work, the group members stated:

a. 'I would say it is definitely an improvement the way it is now. But it depends on solidarity and agreement among those working together. . . The time you save up now, you can use for the common good. . . There is more co-operation among the men, you get more in touch to discuss what is of joint interest. . .'
b. 'I would say this is at least not any worse than before. . . I thought it would be hopeless to get a group willing to work together. . . I must say the attitude is much better at least in our group. . . It was straightforward when you had your own bench but we can easily see now that there is an advantage to switch over to another bench even when it is harder to run it. There is some variation in it. . . I am sure we could get something extra out of it, something that counts, if we stand together as a group. We could make suggestions regarding things on the benches, speed etc. We must run at such a speed that we

feel that we move along with the machine . . . I must say that this system gives some possibilities for increased production. . .'

c. 'Well I thought this was no good. Wire drawing is wire drawing whether you run one bench or the other. . . But now I have seen that it is much better (group work) than it was before. . . I find it better now since there is some more variation and we have more space to move about. And at the same time there is more chance to help each other.'

d. 'Yes, I think there is much more variation, that is important. . . And work is more evenly distributed when some benches are heavier. . . I find this group work OK. . . but at first I had little hope in it. . . There is more variation. . . And we have a better chance to help each other with breakages and things like that.'

Commenting on *social interaction* everyone agreed that group work meant an improvement. A typical statement was:

'First and foremost I would say you find more satisfaction now. There is much more co-operation between the boys. . . And regarding the work there is much better contact.'

Boundary tasks like simple *maintenance* and *training* under the group system of work were not really attempted. But the general opinion was that the group system would open some new possibilities in these respects with mutual advantage to the men and the plant.

2. *Productivity*. Productivity during Phase II is shown below. The results reflect the general conclusion that under optimal conditions the group system would not only give more satisfaction but would also release potential human resources in terms of higher productivity and improved earnings.

Graph III.3. Productivity of experiment benches. Moving averages of 3 shifts.

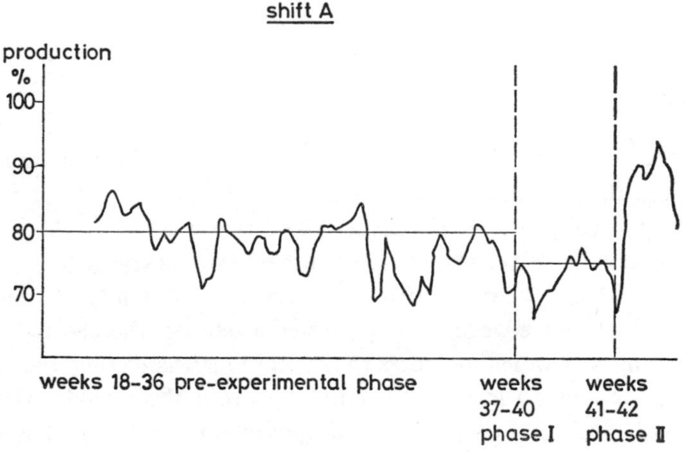

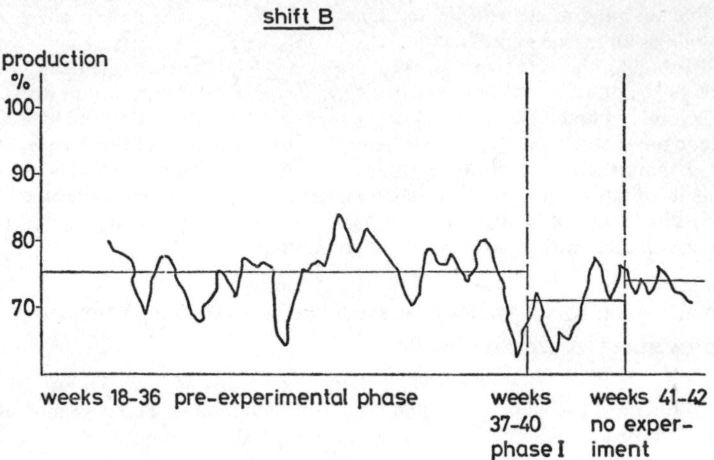

A striking illustration of the psychological unrest caused by the success of weeks 5 and 6 was the circulation in the factory of a rumour to the effect that a foreman had said that this group method was dangerous for the interests of the workers. Such rumours do not spread unless important interests are involved. Investigating this rumour, we found that it arose from a gross distortion of an actual incident. A number of men were looking at the production board and discussing the outstanding achievements of the new group. A foreman who was present asked how they felt about the group system: 'Did they feel that the men in the group were doing *too* well?'

The performance of the volunteer group in this short phase of two weeks was taken by all in the plant as proving that the group method was successful.

3.5.3. Phase III

Literally the experiment was over with the sixth week and for the remainder of the agreed three months period Group A settled back to working so that the status quo would not be threatened. The men worked on the old ratio of one man, one machine. They did not entirely give up trying to exploit the potentiality of the system, but with the time they now had at their joint disposal for productive work, they suggested a scheme whereby they would stagger the times at which members took meal breaks and keep the benches running continuously through the shift. To avoid the trouble with 'rate busting' and earning too much, they proposed that only a part would be taken out in wages; the rest might be taken out by dropping the short Saturday shift and letting some men on the afternoon shift finish early. The experimental conditions agreed upon by management and union did not allow for such changes to take place. Since this was the case, Group A which had experienced the potential incentives in the group system lost interest when these incentives did not exist any more.

The second volunteer group started up on the afternoon shift on 2 November (Monday of the nineth week). They also accepted the tacit restraints on production, but they tried to utilise the potentialities of group work to a much larger extent than Group A after Phase II.

Graph III.4. Productivity of experiment benches. Moving averages (of 3 shifts).

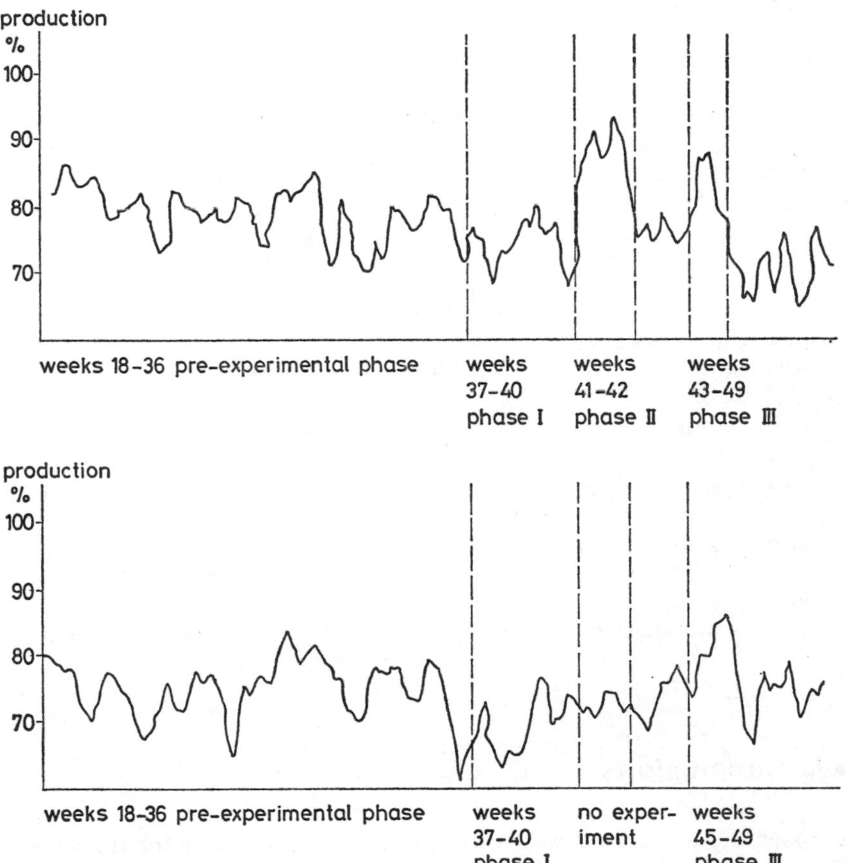

In effect the men accepted that the group system was no longer experimental but could not be developed in practice until the whole problem of wages and employment was subject to new agreements with management. The production records reflect this state of affairs. (See p. 51 for production in Phase III.)

3.6. Some overall measures

3.6.1. Comparison interviews

A week and a half after the experiment was over, the former group members were interviewed briefly about their attitude towards group working as compared to single bench working:

General attitude:				
prefer group	5	neutral 3	prefer single	2
Group work is:				
more interesting	9	neither 1	more boring	0
Group work is:				
more varied	9	neither 1	more monotonous	0
Group work gives:				
less work	4	neither 2	more work	4
Group work situation is:				
more relaxed	3	neither 4	more tense	3
Group work gives:				
less wire breaks	0	neither 6	more wire breaks	4
Group work means:				
less need of maintenance	0	neither 8	more need of maintenance	2
Group work means:				
less contact with foreman	6	neither 3	more contact with foreman	1
Group work means:				
more contact with other workers	9	neither 1	less contact with other workers	0

3.7. Conclusions

Although the experiment went through the formal motions for the agreed three months, it is clear that the reality was quite different. The initial agreement had been reached in an atmosphere of considerable suspicion and mistrust so that, not surprisingly, even the basic conditions were interpreted differently. This atmosphere dominated Phase I but it did not entirely disappear during the remaining course of the experiment. Even when, in Phase II, the operators had proved to their own satisfaction that they could master the group system they then sat back as it were to await negotiation of the rewards. They were not prepared to set new production norms before the new levels of reward were firmly set by negotiation. It should not be thought that the distrust was one-sided nor that it was unusual for an industrial concern of this kind. All that was unusual was the novelty of the experiment. Thus the collaboration of union officials and management seemed strange and aroused suspicions; the presence of research people invoked the more familiar image of managerially oriented consultants; the meetings, votes and requests for volunteers smelt of manipulation in a process traditionally governed by dictates or voting with one's feet: the challenge to a working method apparently dictated by technological necessity just seemed quixotic. These factors as much as the content of the experiment itself occupied the minds of those concerned, supervisors and staff, as well as operators. Unfortunately, they were not conducive to a 'Hawthorne' effect. Instead these factors sustained the fears and concerns of people within the experiment; they mobilized pressures from those other workers in the Department who were outside the experiment but feared the pressure of higher production norms; and they froze off potential areas of support and leadership in other areas.

The main result of the experiment was to demonstrate that *the major difficulty lay not in designing more appropriate work systems but in changing from the old ones.* At least this seemed to be true of technical systems as simple as this and of changes that deliberately sought to involve the willing collaboration of those directly concerned. It was thought possible that in more complex technologies the re-design problems could become paramount, and also possible that change could be easier if simply imposed from above. Thus, as in the case of designing and manning a new production plant union negotiators could take a longer view than can operators imbued with notions of job ownership in an established plant.

The second most important result was the demonstration that *the major difficulty in changing from the old system lay in the very novelty of the exercise.* In a situation where mutual trust existed this would probably not have been so troublesome – if people did not understand they would still be inclined to assume that the change was for the best. However, in this typical industrial situation of the early sixties people started from a position of mutual distrust, even distrusting their union representatives and the willingness of their workmates to collaborate fairly. Thus, any movement by management that smacks of novelty arouses fears of being manipulated in ways for which they may not have prepared defences. The reassurances of trade union officials, from their own shop stewards to the national leaders, could not quieten their uneasy feeling that such men have sold out before. In any case, as we saw here, there was beyond the first line of trade unions defences, a *second line of defences* based on shop floor practices and customs. It was this second line that appeared to be particularly threatened. The existence of this second line of defences had been well documented in previous industrial studies but we must admit to being surprised at their strength, even when the changes were designed to better the position of the operators. We were confronted at many points with the wisdom of the folk saying, 'better the devil you know than the one you don't.'

The third of these unintended results was a little more novel and arose directly from the successful, although limited, achievements of the planned experiment. As expected the operators did eventually see the advantages for them in the new system (Table, p. 52). Furthermore, the system gave clear promise of greater productivity under these conditions of improved working. The operators had little doubt that they could achieve and better the 20 per cent increase in production of Phase II. Joint discussions after the experiment were based on this. However, it soon emerged that what could be done in the wire drawing department could not be divorced from the web of industrial agreements covering the industry and the nation. To pay the men for such an increase in productivity would disrupt the status-payment relations in the industry. Wire drawers might even start to earn as much as top steel-furnace men. This disruption could not be risked by the company nor by the national leaders. The point was taken by the operators who then proposed that their benefit might come from a reduction in working hours. Unfortunately, the question of working hours was under consideration at the national level and the national leaders could not endorse local agreements that jumped the gun. This sealed off developments in the wire drawing department. The Joint Research Committee was satisfied that the experiment had made its point and that the project should proceed whilst they looked more closely at the constraints built into the negotiated effort-reward agreements. The company turned its interest toward parallel developments in other departments. The researchers sought further insights from the observations they were able to make during the experiment. The following points were brought out in the report to the Joint Committee:

Job Content. The group method of working radically improved the activity profile and the men found their work more varied and interesting. Although the men were still learning to work together as a group, it was clear that they had begun to develop an appropriate rhythm in their activity and to co-operate in clearing wire breakages. Not much further improvement in the challenge of the job could be expected until the groups took over responsibility for some of the maintenance tasks.

Training. Training and induction to the old system had been unsatisfactory. It was difficult to prepare a person before putting him onto a machine on his own with all of its attendant difficulties and dangers. Many men left at this stage. In the groups, however, an individual has constant support and guidance and could proceed at his own rate to master the various tasks. Even at the early stages when the person had only mastered such simple tasks as taking off the finished coils he could already pull his weight in the group. Thus in one of the groups a young man with restricted learning abilities was left to take off the coils most of the time. He was happy with his task and proud of his membership in the group. The others were happy to let him do a necessary but, for them, a fairly boring chore.

Supervision. Although it was obvious that the group system would entail new styles of supervision no serious steps were taken to prepare the supervisors. It was felt that this was too much to expect from managment when it was by no means clear that the new styles were going to be needed after the 3 months of experimentation. Close contact with the supervisors during this period gave some idea of the ways in which their role would evolve. The most striking change was in the reduction of time spent in settling down-time problems. In the old system the supervisors were spending about half their time in sorting out what would be a fair allowance for machine down-time due to breakages etc. These problems arose at all sorts of times and constantly disrupted the efforts of supervisors to plan their other tasks. More than that it centred the relations between the operators and supervisors on payment problems, not production problems. With the group system the supervisor was largely freed of these disruptions. His direct dealings with the groups tended to be focussed on discussions with the workers about production problems. The implication of these preliminary observations is that although the groups take over some of the traditional powers of a supervisor (particularly in the hour-to-hour control and co-ordination of individual behaviour), the supervisory role needs to be extended in new directions. In particular the supervisor will need to be trained and empowered to handle most of the planning required to ensure that the group can maintain a smooth continuity in their productive operations planning that is currently done by staff people at least one step removed from the floor. That is, the groups will need someone who is more of a manager than a straw-boss.

Introduction of change. In this experiment every effort was made to minimize unnecessary novelty and hence as much use as possible was made of formal channels of communication. This may or may not have been a mistake. In any case future experiments in the project would not be as novel to unionists or management and it seemed advisable to develop better communications than achieved in the wire mill. An action committee should be formed as soon as all parties have agreed on some concrete proposals for job re-design. The committee should include several representatives from the shop floor, a supervisor and the departmental head. Perhaps a work study man or a training officer could be assigned to aid such a committee. A committee like this could speed up communications and ensure a quicker examination of proposals from many angles. More importantly, it could give the men the assurance that beyond a certain stage the experiment has become *their* experiment, not something imposed and run by outside strangers.

4. The Hunsfos Pulp and Paper Mill

From a list of pulp and paper mills selected by the Joint Committee as suitable for experimentation, the Hunsfos mill emerged as the one best able to start immediately. Hunsfos is in the Vennesla community, on the Otra River, about ten miles north of Kristiansand, in the southernmost part of Norway. Since 1873, it has been the major employer in the community, and as recently as 1963 employed about 50% of the adult male working population. Of the workforce of 900-1,000 persons, about 80% had close links with the local area, and in many cases members of the families had been employed by Hunsfos for three generations.

Thc interpersonal relations at work are stable and closely linked to the religious, political and economic life of the community. Neither the managers nor technical staff are usually recruited from the local district, however, and they can be classified as a distinct social group in the community. Hunsfos, has a strong professional management respected both in the industry and in the plant and strong union leadership with effective working relations with the central union headquarters in Oslo.

The company is fully integrated, and includes the major technologies in the field - mechanical pulping, chemical pulping and papermaking. In 1964, production came to 54,000 tons of paper, and total sales volume was about 80 million Norwegian kroner. The principle steps in the manufacture of paper are preparation of the wood (cutting into proper lengths, barking and chipping), mechanical and chemical pulping (breaking the wood down, mechanically or chemically, into pulp), stock preparation (where the pulp is treated and mixed with other materials), the paper machines (where the pulp, mixed with water, is converted into paper), and the finishing step (supercalendering, cutting, sorting and packing).

4.1. Selection of the Chemical Pulp Department (CPD)

In September 1964, management and the union at Hunsfos agreed to let the research team find an area in the plant to experimentally introduce new principles of job design. To be acceptable, the area would have to have 'process technology' characteristics, and a high potential for diffusion of results to the rest of the company.

After conducting detailed surveys, including extensive employee interviews in a number of departments presenting the desired characteristics, the researchers chose the Chemical Pulp Department. This department appeared to be a 'naturally' bounded socio-technical unit which could be shielded off relatively well from the rest of the company and which possessed a high degree of self-regulation. The department also contained an opportunity for improvement, because quality variations in the timber, if not coped with in chemical pulping, would result in a lower quality (and lower economic value) of the paper. Moreover, because the department was located between the wood preparation and the paper mill, changes in the department's operations could exert maximum leverage on these functions. Finally, local leadership on the management as well as on the union side appeared capable and willing. We expected that this factor would offset the resistance to change that might be expected from the senior operators (ten out of fifteen of whom were over 50) and some of the workers who might stick stubbornly to established ways or attempt to isolate themselves.

4.2. The technical system

The technical system of the Chemical Pulp Department consists of five conversion processes carried out in adjacent areas: *boiling*, *screening*, *bleaching*, *boiling acid preparation*, and *bleaching liquid preparation*. Figure 1 shows a schematic picture of the equipment involved.

First, chips of spruce, fir and hardwood are boiled separately in large digesters with magnesium bisulfite acid. In the wood the two major components, lignin and cellulose, form a rigid structure. Under the right conditions of acid strength, temperature, pressure, and time, the lignin is dissolved and the cellulose fibres are released. The fibres, together with other undissolved material, are prepared for further separation in the screening section; the lignin and the used boiling liquid go to waste. Fresh magnesium bisulfite acid is drawn from a buffer tank, to which acid continuously feeds after it has been prepared from magnesium oxide and sulphur dioxide in a separate section.

A system of screens increases the purity of the fibres by removing unboiled wood particles, small fibre fragments, and other impurities. From the screening, the pulp of spruce goes to buffer storage, while the fir and hardwood are transferred to bleaching. The bleaching liquid, prepared from chlorine and sodium hydroxide, dissolves residual lignin attached to, and discolouring, the fibres. The three pulps together with mechanical pulp are the major raw material for the paper machines.

Thus the CPD appeared to have relatively clear-cut and easily perceived boundaries with the rest of the total production system at Hunsfos. Buffer storage at the input and output ends of the CPD had by 1974 become relatively satisfactory, and therefore the department was felt to be adequately isolated from quantitative disturbances in other departments.

A number of potential technical variations had to be constantly watched and controlled. First, the use of fir as a raw material had led to serious pitch problems. Hence, when sticky resin accumulated in the screening or bleaching, extensive cleaning was required. Variations arising from varied growing and storage conditions were transmitted along with the materials and, if not controlled, could reduce the paper quality. Treating spruce, fir, and hardwood batches in the same equipment induced additional variations due to reciprocal pitch contaminations and mixing of different fibres.

The individual sub-processes were by themselves relatively complex. As they were separated from each other, there were only limited contacts between them. Thus they appeared to form relatively self-sufficient units in themselves. However, a number of important relationships still existed between the sub-processes and across shifts. For example, the boiling and bleaching operations were interdependent, and there was a 16-hour cycle between filling and emptying each of the four boilers, requiring close co-operation across shifts. Finally, it became evident that not all the problems were fully predictable. The resin problem was far from being fully understood and the variations in raw materials made it impossible to predict what problems might come up at any time. Moreover, the properties of the technical equipment could change somewhat over time. This meant that the process control standards were more or less arbitrary and should doubtless be adjusted periodically.

The chemical pulp department

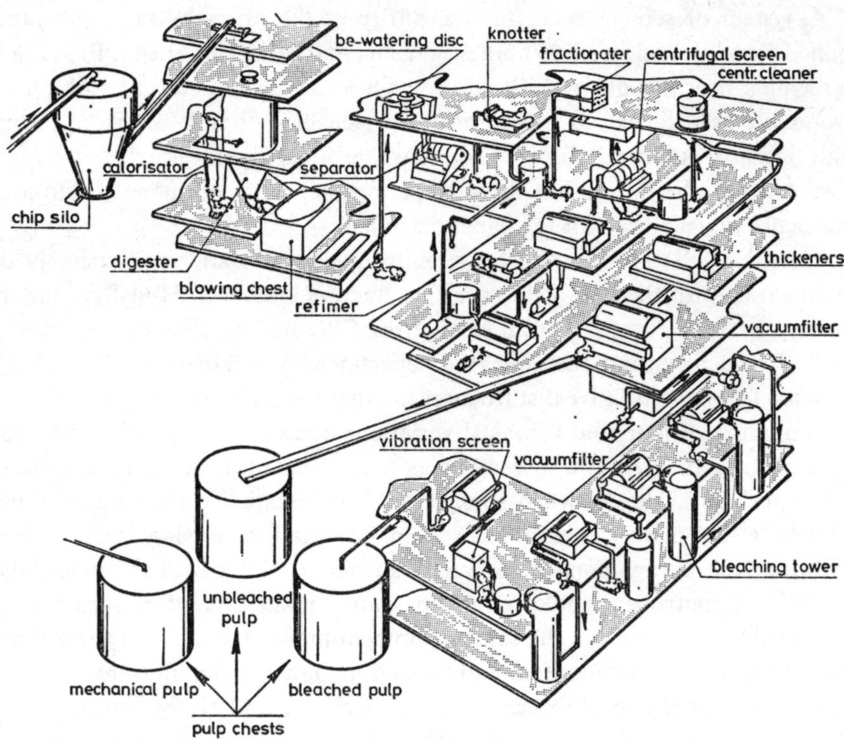

4.3. The social system

The department organization included seven positions and four shift teams, plus one day-shift worker who prepared the bleaching agents – a total of 29 employees. One senior operator was responsible for each of the other four sub-processes on each shift. These men belonged to the higher of the two recognized status levels. The boiler assistant, the screener assistant, and the reserve on each shift, together with the day-shift worker, made up the second status grade. In service roles outside the department were two laboratory technicians providing data for process control. In case of mechanical breakdowns or pitch-troubles the operators had to rely on outside maintenance men and cleaning people. Four shift foremen (plus one assistant foreman to coveı absentees) were responsible for both chemical and mechanical pulping. Above the shift foremen were the general foreman, the production engineer, the pulp mill manager and the general manager.

It should be noted that, in the Norwegian pulp and paper industry, the number of operator positions is strictly prescribed in the central agreement with the union. At Hunsfos this had undoubtedly accentuated the strict delimitation of work between individual jobs. This point is of crucial importance.

The operators' wages consisted of hourly pay, shift allowances, regular overtime, 'additional hours', and production bonus. The complexity of the arrangement made it difficult for the average worker to see any clear relationship between his efforts and his wage.

The production bonus was based on the number of batches of paper produced, even though it was the paper-machines that caused bottlenecks. The CPD operators could facilitate the operation of the paper-machines only by producing higher quality pulp, but this aspect of their work was not considered in the bonus. This was an unfortunate omission, because management was at that time extremely anxious to build the company's quality reputation. Through a quality bonus, it could easily have translated this company goal into operational terms at the lower levels.

The 'additional hours' segment of the wage was a form of extra pay for odd jobs carried out, not in overtime, but during regular working hours. It reflected management's efforts to cope with the lack of flexibility on the shop floor.

Operator training was limited by the traditional notion of 'one man, one job'. Hence, when a man had been selected for one department, advancement was confined to jobs in the same area.

The segregation of jobs and lack of overlapping skills in the shift teams made it increasingly difficult to cope with variations in the process. A multi-skilled reserve had been introduced on each shift to stand in for absentees and help out with odd jobs. Unfortunately, the imbalance between the high skills required for the job, and the pay, security, and working conditions offered, was so great that the position was not sought after and there was a high turnover among the reserves.

Traditionally, management has seen apparent advantages in strict delineation of individual jobs. Training time is short and supervisory control is strong. But workers tend to react by regarding the job specifications as the maximum they owe rather than the minimum. Thus we could observe that, in the CPD, the men were using the rigid job specifications as a defense against management action. Moreover, they had created a 'pecking order' among themselves based on what were considered the more cushy jobs and the less attractive ones.

Consequently, while a job may lack intrinsic satisfaction, it may acquire psychological significance only because of *relative* advantages of a rather marginal nature. Moreover, as the men come to judge themselves and others on their ability to seize these relative advantages, they become strong defenders of the system despite its built-in limitations for self-fulfilment.

As an example of the insidiousness of this system, our post hoc analysis of the batch records revealed that one of the four digestors was an unusually good piece of equipment for preparing a certain type of wood, but this fact was not generally known. However, it appeared that one of the boilermen had discovered this some time previously and had kept it to himself. This suggests not only that the lack of learning was due to feelings of complacency or uncertainty among the men, but that the system failed to encourage the men to share self-acquired knowledge, because they did not consider themselves as members of a cohesive group sharing common goals.

Our analysis showed that the main lacks in the jobs were of the interest, excitement and self-enhancement that comes from being able to learn to do a task better. On the other hand, the degree of variety and challenge and scope for personal control were higher than usual in industrial jobs and were felt to be so by the operators.

This explains the relatively high degree of job satisfaction expressed by senior operators, who had little reason to desire a learning process that might disturb some of their privileges. However, the assistants and the reserves expressed a lower level of satisfaction.

The shift foremen in the CPD had been introduced as a management response to variation problems arising after a changeover to the magnesium bisulfite method. This response was in accordance with the traditional answers to organizational problems on the shop floor, which include such measures as specifying individual jobs in more detail, strengthening supervision, calling in specialists, and introducing a new level in the organization. In this case a short-term solution was achieved by creating a more serious long-term problem.

Recruited from among the best operators, the foremen could only with extensive training achieve a real leadership position clearly above the operator group. Familiar with operator work and lacking the means to lift himself to a new level, the foreman tended to concentrate on the work group rather than on controlling its 'boundary conditions'. He was constantly on the move as a trouble shooter, doing most of the unpredictable tasks that the operators were reluctant to carry out without special compensation (under the 'additional hours' arrangement).

The foremens' behaviour became part of the 'vicious circle' of job segregation by further limiting the learning and growth potentials of the operators. As the first level of management was in this way lowering itself to fill in within its area of command, so each higher level was correspondingly pulled down to fill in the lacks below. The adverse consequences of such work organization at the floor level will easily affect all levels of management, a situation typical of large organizations. At Hunsfos, these tendencies were evident. Managers and foremen were subtly redefining their own jobs in a way that reinforced the reluctance of the men on the floor to show more initiative than was demanded by the traditional job design. Thus the 'vicious circle' was established and maintained.

4.4. Improving conditions for personal participation

The Hunsfos mill was selected as a site for an industrial democracy experiment in February 1964. This event was followed by more than six months of discussion among the management, the trade union, and members of the research team, who made a number of visits to the plant. At this point, top management felt the experiment offered an interesting challenge, but also felt some apprehension over possible unrest and a possible weakening of the positions of supervisors and staff. The union leaders felt that changes were necessary and were eager to pioneer in efforts to democratize the work place, but felt quite unsure about the direction.

At a joint meeting attended by both workers and management representatives in September 1964, it was agreed that the research team would make a sociotechnical study of the company to select an experimental site. In order to protect the interests of all parties, it was agreed that the project would progress step by step, would be evaluated after each step, and could be stopped completely after any particular phase by either management or the workers. Through the following February, the research team worked intensively in gathering and analysing data and in building channels of communication to all levels of the company. Activities included interviews, meetings, and the study of written statements and statistics. Weekly reports were made to the personnel manager and the chief shop steward.

Top management became, during this phase, more interested when data in areas of particular importance to them (mainly production problems) were brought up for discussion. Middle managers in general were sceptical since they saw the project as strengthening workers' positions and weakening their own – though a few managers saw the long-term prospects for the development of all employees, and took a more positive attitude. The union began to get a clearer idea of what the project might involve and was surprised to find that top management was willing to work along these lines. Some hope was expressed that problems basic to the future of the union could, with the help of the project, be transmitted up from the company level to central LO headquarters. The local shop stewards continued to co-operate and were eager to discuss production problems that were relevant to them.

In February, 1965, in separate meetings, labour and management accepted the research team's recommendation following its study of the plant – that the experimental project begin in the Chemical Pulp Department. During the following two months, a number of search meetings were held with the CPD management, foremen, operators and laboratory technicans. Supplementary data were collected to serve for a more detailed analysis of the department.

It was at this point that difficulties began to appear. The manager of the CPD, who by then was the strongest supporter of the project among all of the middle managers, decided to leave the company for personal reasons. In addition, some incidents regarding personnel policy in other departments had some negative effects on operator attitudes in the CPD. The union support continued strong, and became actively involved when some operators proved unwilling to participate in search activities. Foremen displayed interest as well as resistance; in general, they withheld personal commitment.

In the research team's analysis of the department, some key areas came to light which, it was felt, could be of great importance in operationalizing the goals of the total organization – that is, expressing those goals in concrete, operational terms at the lowest level of the socio-technical system. One such area was *process control* which is intended to achieve for each product a given set of quality specifications, minimizing hours, cost of material, labour cost, and the like. Another area was *production planning* which aims at achieving optimal allocation of products and orders, and considering market requirements as well as production costs.

In process control, a vital element is a flow of information which must cover a network of interdependencies and stimulate responses in the social system. Generally speaking, a self-regulating production system requires (1) *a production unit*, (2) *an output standard* against which the output can be judged, (3) *a measuring device* to detect deviations from the output standard and feed the information back to a 'brain' unit, (4) a *'brain' unit* that can translate information received into new instructions to return production to the standard, while also considering current input characteristics, (5) *an operational* unit to carry out the instructions and (6) *an input standard* against which input can be judged and fed forward to the 'brain' unit with information on deviations.

In man-machine systems, human elements will be part of the control, either by performing the component tasks or transmitting information. The effectiveness of feedback loops will depend on the properties of the components and the transmission of information.

In the CPD, the only qualitative measurements being made were of 'degree of digestion,' 'brightness,' and 'tearing strength'. 'Purity' was judged subjectively from test sheets, but factors such as 'pitch' and 'homogeneity' could not be regularly measured economically. There were no measurements on quality of input chips, but information on pH-value and percentage of sulphur dioxide in the acid was available. Because of great variations in individual batch qualities, it was difficult to see long-term trends in process control. The lack of feedback here reduced the opportunities for continuous learning. With some improvements, we felt that these measurements might form the basis of a temporary bonus that might encourage the operators to work toward group goals.

In order to keep feedback loops as short as possible, we felt that information and decisions should be brought to the lowest possible level and kept within the smallest possible number of work roles and levels. Customarily, because of the rigid specification of work roles and authority channels, there is a rather broad span of information flows. The advantage this gives in terms of increased control must be weighed against the defects – delays and misinterpretations of information and also the restricted job satisfaction and motivation that result from the non-unified nature of the jobs in question.

This point was well illustrated in one inadequate feedback loop discovered in the CPD. This concerned the 'purity' of unbleached pulp, a measure of the performance of the screening operation. The sheets were prepared by the laboratory technician about an hour after the screening of a new batch had begun. Instead of returning the sheets immediately to the screener, who could then make the necessary corrections in the process, the laboratory sent them to the foreman and some supervisors in other departments. Since the foreman was frequently away from his office, feedbacks to the operators were often much delayed. There was no question of the operators' ability to interpret the information contained in the test sheets, nor was there any doubt that the other departments would benefit by a change in the procedure. The only defect in the present procedure was in the *speed* of the feedback, which was determined by the broad span of information flow across job roles and status levels.

4.5. Program for change – 'The Easter Document'

After we had finished our analysis of the conditions of production and collaboration, a program of meetings and deliberations was carried out by the workers, supervisors and management in the Chemical Pulp Department. As a result concrete proposals for starting a change process in the CPD, to begin after Easter 1965, was put forward in a joint management union meeting. The so-called 'Easter Document' read as follows:

1. *The purpose* is to improve the conditions of personal participation and daily work with respect to tasks and decision-making. Specific changes in working conditions and managerial practices will be initiated for this purpose. Further measures, for instance, in training, will be initiated as soon as they prove necessary.

2. *The experimental site*, for the time being, is limited to the Chemical Pulp Department. This limitation may seem artificial, but there are several good reasons for it:
a. This kind of experiment could not possibly be carried out unless people involved have the opportunity to test step by step the possible consequences of the experiment.
b. The CPD constitutes a relatively natural unit which can be separated from preceding and subsequent steps in the production process and where it is possible to estimate quantity and quality of inputs and outputs.
c. When experiments have provided a basis for further extension, it will be natural to work from the CPD both to the preceding and subsequent steps of the process line.

3. *Increased autonomy for 'extended groups'* is a plausible label for the principle forming the basis of the experiments. 'Extended' here refers to

groups of workers in the production process that will have to co-operate in an extended geographical area across the shifts. 'Autonomy' refers to the fact that groups of workers will, within given limits, be able themselves to co-ordinate their work and make decisions. The autonomy will be limited by technological and economic demands which have to be met. In addition, the group autonomy has to be adapted to the responsibilities of the foremen, the supervisors and the service departments, in co-ordinating and managing the work and processes of the company as a whole.

4. *The method of carrying out the changes* will be a step by step problem-solving by small groups consisting of representatives from the workers, supervisors, and management. Experts will be consulted according to the character of the tasks and problems. No change will be effected before the people concerned have had an opportunity to express their opinions. No existing area of responsibility will be altered without agreement on the justifiability of the new distribution of responsibility.

5. *There are certain pre-requisites* for the development of partly 'autonomous' work groups in the CPD (among others):

a. Specification of the groups' 'boundaries' in relation to the environment (adjacent units).
b. Clarification and definition of *what* has to be measured in terms of quality and quantity of raw materials and services both received and delivered by the group.
c. Specification of quality control limits for the various criteria (or measures) the group would have to meet concerning control of the process.
d. A proper group incentive, eventually a bonus, which can stimulate the group to co-operate. (Any ultimate settling of a prospective bonus will take place in the usual way by negotiation.) (If a new bonus is to be set up, it ought to be based on such criteria that everybody has a clear understanding that the group positively *can* effect these criteria. Measurable improvements in quality (or noticeable improvements) in utilisation of raw materials, chemicals, and equipment are good examples of a sound basis for group bonus. A possible bonus system must not be allowed, however, to artificially isolate the CPD from other departments, or must not prevent the changeover to a common bonus system for the whole process line at a later date.)

6. *Preliminary group activity* will consist of meetings of workers whose tasks

are interdependent, their supervisors, and eventually the researchers, to co-operate in the solution of tasks mentioned above in section 5. This is an important means of increasing the personal participation and autonomy in the production group. The workers will be consulted when the measures mentioned in section 7 below, are to be worked out. As the group of operators jointly takes over responsibility, it is probable that the division of labour, and thence individual jobs, will be modified according to the needs of the group as a whole.

7. *Other measures that support* the group arrangement will be carried out by the management:

a. CPD will have its own repairman who is to co-operate directly with the operators and the supervisors.
b. The system of greasing will be improved.
c. Training of operators to make them qualified for all tasks within the department will be tried out for those who need and wish it.
d. An 'information centre' will be established where measurements and other information are quickly available so that everyone will be up-to-date with the situation in the department.
e. The conditions will be suitably arranged so that employees of the department can meet in small or larger groups when necessary (among other things, in connection with the accomplishment of measures mentioned in section 5 above).
f. The necessary telephones will be installed to facilitate communication among the sub-sections of the department.

8. *The local trade union* will also take some measures to support and facilitate the development of group autonomy.

a. One worker in each shift on the CPD is elected as a representative to meet the researchers, management, and the local trade union while the experiments are in progress. (One of the shift contact men will be the main contact man in the department.)
b. The trade union will try to clarify what consequences these new ideas being tried out in the Industrial Democracy Project at Hunsfos will have on the future role of the local trade union. (Will there be, as in the case of 'work study representatives', need of 'specialist representatives' who 'can help with the design' of good jobs? How are worker representatives to co-operate on these questions among different companies and among different branches?)
c. In addition, the leaders of the local trade union, in the same way as the

management of the company, will have to take charge of the negotiable problems as they arise.

9. *The role played by the research team* with respect to the experiment will be to:
a. Record the effects of the experiments.
b. Give counselling assistance in the carrying through of concrete measures.
c. Play an active role in the development of concrete measures whenever, in the opinion of both parties, it is necessary in order to keep within the project's time limit.

10. *The responsibility* rests with management for the accomplishment of the various measures mentioned in section 7 and the responsibility for those mentioned in section 8 with the local trade union. The researchers must not, under any circumstances, interfere with the responsibility that the management and the local trade union have in their respective area. This applies also to measures mentioned in sections 5 and 6, where composite groups – if necessary with active co-operation from the researchers – will work out suggestions for solutions.

11. *The measures now initiated have to be regarded as an experiment* and the parties are not bound to continue after the results are evaluated by September 1st, 1965, at the latest. The management and the local trade union must agree about prolongation of the arrangements resulting from the experiments beyond this time limit.

4.6. From information to involvement – 'The Easter Document'

One might say that the social process of the experiment turned from 'exchange of information' to 'active involvement' when the Easter Document proposals were presented to a joint meeting on the 28th April 1965. Representatives of management and the union agreed to the proposal, on conditions that the research team would play an active part in carrying it out. The union also made its approval contingent on the willingness of the men in the department to accept it. The men did indeed vote to accept it, but a vocal minority insisted the vote was not valid because not everyone was present. Another vote was organised. Though the proposal carried only by a single vote, the union decided that the experiment should go on.

In this period we were confronted with a manifestation of suspicion and hostility among the operators that was somewhat unexpected. However, the fears that develop when novel changes are proposed might seem surprising unless it is remembered that important aspects of individuals' lives are being tampered with. In a situation like this, it is understandable that the parties concerned have little real reason to believe that the researchers know what it means to be in the position of a worker, foreman or even manager, and they have equally little reason to believe that social scientists are influenced by values that are acceptable to the parties involved.

At a meeting with the CPD people in July, the general manager gave assurances that no reduction in the workforce would take place during the experiment, and representatives of the national employers' and union organizations also voiced their support. After this, opposition among operators was reduced to a small, though vocal, minority.

Concrete changes made during this period included adding a local repair man to the CPD, installing the promised telephones, and introducing a better information system. Though the research team was pushing ahead, progress was still not felt to be satisfactory, and it became clear that management would have to participate more actively. Management accepted this and suggested allocating special people to take care of this.

At the evaluation meeting scheduled for September, all parties agreed that the changes made so far were insufficient, and that further measures were needed. Opposition to the project was vociferously offered, but an open discussion led to concrete discussions and some constructive suggestions. It was agreed that an Action Committee, consisting of the training officer, the assistant foreman, and a bleacher operator, would be set up to stimulate the growth of local initiative. The Committee would maintain close contact with all parties concerned.

4.7. Local initiative – 'The Action Committee'

The operators' acceptance of the Action Committee was the first solid indication that they wanted to go ahead.[1] Top management demonstrated its

1. Our previous studies had shown the majority of the men to be interested in experimenting along the proposed lines, but, until now, their respect for the interest of the small minority of vociferous opponents had been the overriding factor. By establishing the Action Committee, the majority announced that they intended to go ahead with the experiment. But they were still ready to take care of the real (not the imaginary) interests of the minority in case of potential conflict.

commitment by financing and helping to man the Action Committee. Middle management became increasingly involved. Foreman were cautiously favourable.

A precondition for the men's co-operation with the Committee was the withdrawal of the research team from the forefront. This was readily complied with; whatever the groundwork we had put in, the experiment had to be theirs and managements, if the men were to gain the assurance and self-confidence needed for any later move from experimentation to implementation.

A second precondition for the men to co-operate was an assurance that the Action Committee was committed to the jointly agreed Easter Document, and not to some covert management scheme. The composition of the Action Committee might have encouraged this anciety. There were agreed ground rules to protect the interests of all parties, but the Action Committee also had its middle management and foremen members. Their role was essentially that of resource people, not representatives. That is, their job was to provide knowledge and skills that the men needed, but did not yet possess. The Committee members apparently had little difficulty in seeing this as their role and rapidly met the challenge as to their impartiality.

The challenge came, in fact, in the first month of the Committee's existence. The men were objecting to a suggestion for job rotation which threatened the relative status of the senior operators within the shift, and hence they opposed the rewarding of multiple skills. The Action Committee met this challenge and worked out with the men an agreement to a training scheme which would improve *intrashift* flexibility not involving *routine* rotation of jobs. There was general acceptance of the notion that the shift should be sufficiently skilled to absorb the temporary absence of any one man. Training for this started in November 1965.

During this period, a number of suggestions came from the men as well as from others for improving various aspects of the technology. As an example, the men initiated the newly designed batch information system modified to allow a better overall representation of the movement of the batches through the various work stations. The rate flow was slow enough to make it better that the flow be represented by movement of cards from position to position on a large board in the information centre rather than physically moving them from post to post along the process line. There were, however, several other suggestions:

The boilermen requested and got a telephone link with the operator in the chip department, so that they could better control their chip supplies.

The 'side relief' of the digestors was changed to allow the acid strength to be increased in the acid house before the liquor was returned to the digestors. This would make it easier for the boilermen to control their process. On the screens extra valves were installed to increase control over pulp flows. The picture that emerged from these early discussions with management and the operators about the screening revealed that quite extensive modifications needed to be worked out systematically rather than piecemeal. This would involve the engineers and technologists and could not be done in time for the start of the experiment. In the bleaching section many suggestions were made throughout this period. These included relating controls and instruments so that they could be effectively used, installation of an alarm that would enable a quick response to lack of bleach, and new controls that would enable the screens to be properly cleaned without stopping all operations.

4.8. Towards commitment to 'the quality bonus'

The most difficult task for the Action Committee during this preparatory phase was the design of a bonus system that would knit the workers together as a group. The importance of this point refers back to the basic assumption of the experimental design expressed in the Easter Document; i.e. the new principles of job design would lead to an optimum socio-technical system in the Chemical Pulp Department only if:

1. the men as a *group* took greater responsibility for operation of the department as a whole, and
2. they were enabled, and initially *encouraged*, to increase their understanding and control of the processes.

These aims were agreed upon by the union and the local management, who had accepted not to use the experimental conditions as an excuse to reduce the manning.[2] The men could not be expected to assume additional responsibilities, and they made it clear they had no intention of doing so, unless new learning and new instrumentation helped reduce uncontrolled variations in the department.

Our analysis showed there were clear possibilities for continuous learning and therefore continuous increases in understanding and control, provided

2. This is an example of temporarily 'shielding' of an experiment before joint experiences and learning can make a solid basis for negotiating the new conditions.

the men could act as a *group* and could study the process as a whole. But until the men could take such a broad view of their task interdependencies as a matter of course, it seemed necessary to artificially emphasise them through a group bonus.

The key problem was to ensure that the bonus did not simply become an incentive to work harder. Because we wanted to enhance the motivational forces arising from the *intrinsic* characteristics of the work, we had to supply an incentive to work in *different* ways. This scheme would define group boundaries and interdependencies and provide the knowledge of results that was essential to learning. Therefore, the bonus should be *minimal*, and probably *temporary*. It had to be based on factors which were significant for company objectives and which the operators could in fact influence (quality, not quantity).

It was agreed to use a bonus-formula which aimed at optimizing kappa number and brightness, and maximizing cleanliness and tearing strength. The factors were assigned different weight according to type of work and the bonus could not exceed 5% of total earnings. The quality factors are measurable and interrelated and to some extent involve all the operating roles. In order to quantify cleanliness-factor, which carried the heaviest weight in the scheme, a new method of spot counting was introduced. Since the bonus could not be related to all the relevant quality and cost factors it would, for the time being, be up to management to watch these and if necessary to issue regulations.

During the bonus discussions it was agreed that the major objective was to get a more *even* pulp quality, and not to seek top results on just some of the factors, and the union suggested that a reduction in the number of 'extremely bad batches' ought to be specially rewarded. Though the bonus was established on a more general basis, this suggests that the operators were particularly concerned about improving the poorest batches.

The workers engaged in much heated discussion on the bonus proposal, resolutely sticking to the Action Committee scheme and opposing management's suggested modifications which would have made the system more complex.

The strong feeling expressed led us to believe, at first, that we had underestimated the significance the workers attached to the bonus as an incentive. That it was, in fact, only a final testing out of management's backing for the principles of the experiment became clear, when four weeks later, the men suggested change in the payment of the bonus, i.e. to be accumulated and paid out half-yearly.

One might conclude that by the introduction of the bonus system on

January 24th, 1966, the conditions of the experiment had according to the program reached full realization. This had been achieved through a process of learning where the men, from a position of (positive and negative) involvement had gradually committed themselves to the experimental aims.

4.9. The experiment evolves through phases of 'search', 'growth' and 'plateau'

In the first period after the bonus went into effect, operator training was accomplished, the information system functioned well, and the allocation of a local maintenance man to the operator groups worked satisfactorily. However, the efforts of the operators at this point did not result in the expected rise in the quality bonus. The reason was that the important cleanliness factor was decreasing, though tearing strength was improving. Cleanliness was declining because the mill was having to use poor-quality imported spruce, and periodic intakes of fresh fir added to the normal pitch problems. These problems, however, created interest among the operators in the technical conditions of process control and induced *search* efforts in a problem area normally watched by managers and engineers. Questions from the men about improvements in technical equipment and work methods were now brought up through the Action Committee, and were considered in meetings between management, foremen, and operators. This led to a stronger management commitment to the project.

Beginning in the summer of 1966, when the mill again began to use more normal raw materials, the men experienced the growth effect that the multiple experimental conditions had been intended to achieve. The operators, who could now better control the process, saw that their increased interest, training and co-operation gave results in terms of quality and bonus. The actual pay out of the rather small bonus accumulated the first half year, nevertheless strengthened their confidence in management's sincerity in the project. Finally, the holiday schedule, usually a source of problems, was worked out very smoothly, giving a concrete demonstration of the value of multiple skills.

The Action Committee was formally dissolved before summer vacation, but its members were to play important roles as resource persons during the autumn. The main task then was to replace the temporary functions of the Action Committee by more direct co-operation between the department management and the operator groups. The men were invited to take an active part in solving problems. Acceptable solutions were found to the problems of allocating cleaning tasks among the men, scheduling the winter holidays and other concrete questions. The operators became interested in cost reductions and the integration between maintenance and operations.

At the end of 1966, the project was not being followed up as planned, and signs of a plateau effect became evident. In spite of preliminary work done by the laboratory, process data were not being returned to the operators for use in further learning. Adjustments in information and bonus systems were not made when the needs arose. The question of increased integration of maintenance, a matter of company policy, was not worked through. The frequency of shift meetings decreased, and the operators once more felt that decisions concerning them were being taken 'over their heads'. In addition, the men now got a well-founded suspicion that management was planning a reduction in the workforce. The department workforce had, in fact, already been reduced when the permanent reserves in the department were made permanent step-ins also for the whole pulp mill. The operators had accepted this, but when later they got the impression that management was doing 'hidden' work studies in order to abolish an assistant operator job, they reacted so strongly that the union had to intervene. In addition, there was growing dissatisfaction with the CPD wages, which had gotten out of step with the paper mill.

Some of these developments can be understood by looking at changes in the company's situation. In autumn 1966, the company's market position became more difficult, and major changes were made in the paper mill to shift toward products with a higher conversion value. By early 1967, management had to concentrate their resources on technical and marketing problems, giving the industrial democracy project less priority. Hence the Action Committee was prematurely discontinued, hampering the process of learning and adjustment on the supervisory and managerial levels in the CPD.

For the sake of interpretation it has to be remembered that these were the circumstances when the men were interviewed about their project experiences, which is part of our analysis in the following section.

4.10. Experimental results in the CPD[3]

4.10.1. Improved pulp quality

The experiment was designed in such a way that pulp quality as measured by the bonus would be the best single index of operator performance. It is agreed within the company that a general improvement in pulp qualities has been achieved (Table 1). This applies to the bleached pulps in particular. In line with this, the number of extremely bad batches have also been reduced during the experiment. For the majority of the individual quality variables (for each pulp), there appears to be some correspondence between quality achieved and the changes in the conditions for operator participation.

Table IV.1. Average quality bonus per week and per batch across all types of timber related to half-year periods of the experiment.

Period	Average week	Average batch
First half-year	100 per cent	100 per cent
Second half-year	145 per cent	140 per cent
Third half-year	124 per cent	137 per cent
Fourth half-year	124 per cent	123 per cent

This broad picture of the bonus trend is confirmed by the more detailed breakdown on pulp qualities.

Before inferring too much from these broad indices, we had to explore whether:

1. the improved quality was achieved at excessive costs.
2. The improved quality was due to improved performance on the group level.
3. There was some evidence that the men took a greater interest in their work.
4. The improvement could have occurred without the men changing their approach to the job.
5. The men themselves perceived the new situation as favourable.

3. A complete version of the analysis of the CPD experiment has already been published (Engelstad, 1970).

4.10.2. Cost trends

There is no evidence that quality has been achieved at the expense of an increased consumption of material resources. The major costs (fibre, yield, chemicals and machine utilisation) that had shown decreasing trends before the experiment, continued to fall during the experiment (Table 2). There is, in fact, some indication that the experiment may have contributed to an increase in yield. It was agreed that manning levels should be kept constant during the experiment. This was done but there was a marked reduction in the involvement of the reserve operators, a shift foreman in the work of this Department and a marked reduction in the so-called 'additional hours' payments.

Table IV. 2. Measures of cost of various materials before and during the experiment.

Material	Nine month period before experiment	12th month period during experiment	% improvement
Magnesium oxide per ton of pulp	106.0	91.0	14.0
Chlorine per ton of pulp	87.3	73.5	15.8
Sulphur dioxide per ton of pulp	128.0	123.0	3.9
Pulp yield per m^3 timber	100.0	103.8	3.8

4.10.3. Emergence of group strategies

The improved control of pulp quality can to a large extent be ascribed to the men who as a group assumed greater responsibility.

1. The quality development of the main product (fir pulp), which goes through all steps in the process, also the bleaching, shows a clear improvement in cleanliness and tearing strength (Table 3). At the same time, the changes in the kappa number show that the boilermen have changed their strategy from overcooking to undercooking, whereas the changes in brightness shows that the bleachers have moved from underbleaching to overbleaching.

The terms underbleaching and overbleaching are to be understood as relative to the given standards for kappa number and brightness, respectively. Nevertheless, these standards are arbitrary ones based on current knowledge and judgement about what would be required to achieve a given pulp quality with the available raw materials, technical equipment and labour force.

A detailed analysis of the situation revealed that these trends in pulp quality could be explained only if the operators, on the basis of the new conditions established, had to some extent changed their attitudes towards the task and their way of working. From previously seeking to optimise within their own delineated work area, therefore, it appeared to be a change in orientation towards optimising on department level, which required an increasing awareness of the technical interdependencies between the part-processes (for example, the removal of lignin in cooking and bleaching, respectively). In other words, the operators now tended to take responsibility as a group.

This conclusion was supported by measurable changes in the pattern of communications and the increased problem-solving activities in the work groups.

Table IV.3. Bonus as a percentage of the theoretical maximum for purity and tearing strength.

Quality dimension	Type of wood	Phase		
		Search	Growth	Plateau
Cleanliness	Fir	42	61	60
(Spots)	Hardwood	45	53	53
	Spruce	3	21	10
Tearing	Fir	63	90	71
Strength	Hardwood	76	96	93

2. Analysis of the communication data shows that the flows of information after the experiment match the technical interdependencies in the process more closely than before. At the same time, the men as a group have attained a higher level of autonomy. It also appears that the assistant operators have now become better integrated into the groups. Table 4 shows that the increased interaction in 1967 in all essentials refers to the substantial growth in interoperator communication (+ 70 per cent).

3. Concrete examples of operator participation in problem-solving and decision making within the department during the experiments also indicate that the men have increased their capability to operate as a team.

Table IV.4. Number of contacts per shift before and after the experiment.

Contact	1965	1967	Difference, per cent	% 1965	% 1967
Operator/operator	26.0	44.1	+70	25	34
Lab. technician/operator	37.7	37.7	0	36	30
Foreman/operator	34.6	39.4	+14	33	31
Foreman/Lab. technician	7.6	6.7	+13	7	5
Total	105.9	127.9	+21	101	100

4.10.4. Operator interest in their jobs

The operators have, during the period of the experiment, contributed a great many suggestions for improvement of the technical equipment and the working condition in general, demonstrating an interest in the job that they previously had not shown (Table 5). At the same time, the operators have become more interested in problems of process control, timber utilisation and costs. Compared with the 53 adopted suggestions in 1966 the formal company suggestion scheme had yielded an average of only one per year, 1958-64.

Obviously, factors other than those included in the experimental design may have contributed to these improvements. It is unlikely, however, that the improved performance gained in the department during the experiment can be assigned to unilateral management actions (regardless of operator response) either in terms of the technical improvements introduced or in terms of the directives given. Indications of this were the lack of pressure from the men before the experiment for improvements in equipment or instrumentation and the fact that when management's major concern in the

Table IV. 5. Number of suggestions advanced and accepted in the operator meetings.

Date of Meetings	Shifts	Acid	Boiling	Screening	Bleaching	Total
15 March 1966	3 + 4	5	5	11	3	24
25 March 1966 (additional)	1 + 2	1	9	3	3	16
August 1966	1+2+3+4	2	4	3	4	13
Total		8	18	17	10	53

summer 1966 turned to input costs, this had no effect on the strategies being followed by the operators in the department. As far as our evidence goes, the improved control, the increase in operator suggestions and other changes in group activities were primarily due to the voluntary efforts of the men.

4.10.5. Operator views on the experiment

No doubt the experiment as it developed in 1966 caused many operators to build up considerable expectations and the feelings of disappointment that were brought out in some of the interviews clearly refer back to the fact that the project was in 1967 only half-heartedly followed up in the department because of other priorities. Unfortunately, at this crucial point in the experiment, new measures necessary to sustain growth in the desired direction, that many had hoped for, were not introduced. In accordance with the logic of systems, it is unlikely that changes in a part will be sustained over an extended period if the changes are not reciprocated by sufficient adjustments in the total system. Within areas where permanent learning has taken place or new technological conditions have been established, however, the socio-technical system in the department appears to have reached a new level of functioning. This applies to pulp quality, operator skill and the degree of flexibility in the shift teams.

In May 1967 we managed to interview 22 out of the 26 operators about their attitudes to the experiment. This systematic study was done because there were some signs of operators being concerned about middle management's apparent attitude and some expressions of the view that their pushing on with the experiment might not be worth the candle.

Despite these forebodings, the results were a shock. We expected a gradation of attitudes because some operators had obviously done better than others from the reorganization; gained more from multi-skilling and more from co-ordination of the work. The results showed a marked polarity. Some of those who in 1965 saw no good coming out of it for them, mainly the boiling men, were now adamant that no good was coming out of it for anyone. They granted that the specific changes in co-ordination, training, flexibility and maintenance were good things. However, the moment a question touched on the general achievments of the project they reacted negatively. This was not simply a matter of sticking to old attitudes. Originally resistance and support had been organized along shift lines. Now this was not so. Originally resistance was organized along the status line between senior operators and assistants. Now it was not. The core of dissatisfaction was with the boiler men, now all of near equal status.

Admittedly they had a bone of contention. None of the suggestions for helping them to better understand and control the digestion process had been accepted. Management, in 1966, had not found the proposals as economically attractive as other current proposals.

However, we looked more carefully as it seemed there might be more to it. Their job position was unique. They were at the front of the chain of interdependencies in the department. What they did (or were thought to do) could be adversely commented on downstream by screeners and bleachers; but not vice versa. By being deprived of what they thought to be necessary instrumentation on their own input of wood chips they were also left open to blame for variances beyond their control. The increased co-ordination within the department had not made their job easier but laid them open to more criticism. Others, not they, benefitted. To overcome this situation they would have needed the knowledge and information flows to enable them to increase their control over digestion, to be able to point out what were not their errors and to take some pride in what were their achievements.

4.11. Towards a further democratization of the company organization

4.11.1. The 1967 Company policy review on the CPD experiment

The CPD experiment at Hunsfos had several aims. It was designed to test new job design principles and, if successful, to serve as a demonstration site for the company, for the pulp and paper industry and for Norwegian industry as a whole. As will be seen, the experiment to a large extent fulfilled these aims in spite of the fact that the CPD team proved unable to sustain its high level of participation of the year 1966.[4]

However, certain tendencies in diffusion suggested that the conditions

4. The experiences from a number of similar change projects in a broad range of industrial companies suggest that there are special difficulties in creating a self-sustaining process of growth within a single part of the system without adequate supporting adjustments on company level, given that the principle of organizational design introduced in the part is fundamentally different from the principle which historically has guided the design and development of the company organization (e.g. based on 'redundancy of functions' versus 'redundancy of parts' which might in our terms also be referred to as the 'democratic' versus the 'bureaucratic' design principles (See Emery 1967).

for our entry into Hunsfos were somewhat inadequate. The management accepted to provide an experimental worksite in the national interest. Neither they nor us pressed the point of what the company would do if the outcome were successful. Contact with the parallel developments in the Shell Refineries (UK) brought home the principle that *a part of a system only influences other parts through its effect on the total system.* The relevance of this principle at plant level became evident by 1967 as a result of the researchers' involvement in both projects and visits by Shell management and union officials.

Hunsfos' management responded quickly although the company was much occupied at the time with developing new market strategies. Hence the first steps toward diffusion to other parts of the company were planned in the paper mill in late 1966. Top and middle management had several conferences to explore the job design principles tested in the CPD and the management principles that were to guide all parts of the company. An agreement was reached:

1. To implement the new principles of job design in the 'paper machines 3-4' department of the Paper Mill.
2. To involve key people in management along one of the production lines to translate the new policy into operational terms.

The first of these decisions was acted upon successfully as reported below. The second turned out to require a long and slow process of development.

In June, 1967, the top management of Hunsfos, with some assistance from the researchers, tried to make explicit what the ID project meant as company policy. A policy document was drafted by the managing director and circulated for discussion among all members of management and staff above supervisory level. Personnel and organisational problems were related to critical interrelations between the company and different markets and institutions. It was concluded that the new ideas tested in the first field experiment (i.e. the Chemical Pulp Department) seemed to be in line with future trends in the society in general and in the Hunsfos environment in particular. The reactions of the members of management were recorded by the researchers and reported to the entire management group. There was general acceptance of the new philosophy but almost no ability to translate the policy into action on the level of production management. It was concluded that top management would have to spend much more time than before on problems of middle management and staff involvement in this new form of organisational development.

4.11.2. Increasing group autonomy in the PM 3-4 department

The new PM 3-4 projcct began in the autumn of 1967. Developments in the CPD by then showed signs of stagnation, and further activities were no longer considered to be part of an experiment under the surveillance of the research team. In PM 3-4 initial consultations with the researchers had taken place the preceding spring, but this time the project was conducted jointly by the management and the union, keeping interferences of outsiders at a minimum. When management in September proposed to implement new design principles in PM 3-4 the idea was supported by all four shift groups.

It was agreed to set up a Project Action Committee consisting of the department superintendent, one assistant foreman and one senior machine operator and each shift group appointed their 'link-man' to facilitate project information across shifts. The CPD experiment was perceived not to be fully successful and may be also too much the researchers' 'baby'. For these and other reasons it could not be just imitated.[5]

The strategy of the PM 3-4 Action Committee was to dissociate psychologically from the previous experiment, yet its members paid attention to the experiences made. Hence, the CPD experiment had made clear that the *traditional* role of the shift foreman seriously inhibited the autonomous functioning of the operator team, and the specific characteristics of the PM 3-4 technology suggested that the men could almost certainly learn to run the department without shift foremen. The foremen were informed about this possibility, but management made it quite clear that possible changes in the foreman role should result in no reductions in either workforce or wages. It should be noted that the tradition of effective communications through the hierarchy of the Paper Mill organization formed a reasonable basis for mutual trust among the parties involved.

By the beginning of 1968 the Action Committee had worked on three main problems:

1. The identification of the most natural boundaries of the PM 3-4 department as a socio-technical unit.
2. The allocation of tasks between the shift foreman and operators as well as management and service positions.
3. The necessary training of operators to work without foremen.

5. In addition to obvious differences between the CPD and the PM 3-4 in tasks, technology and work organization, socio-technical change is a *process* which involves learning through participation. In principle this type of change cannot be copied in the same way as can changes in technology.

There appeared to be two tasks – the preparation of glue and the clay storage – that formally belonged to the department without being neither geographically nor technologically closely related to PM 3 and 4 operations. Since these tasks induced variations in manning difficult to master autonomously for the groups working the paper machines, they were transferred to other departments. It was found that the functions of the shift foreman covered about 30 tasks. Suggestions were worked out in order to simplify the work (time journal, information board etc.), and to distribute the various tasks among the operators (colouring of paper), the foreman (recording of working hours, pay). To give the group sufficient flexibility to cope with variations in production, absenteeism and holidays, a plan for multi-job training was worked out. The system of having one permanent stand-in was then discontinued. With a temporary intake of two extra operators the training program, including a special course in colouring the paper was carried though in spring 1968.

Most of the operators got involved in the project through a series of shift meetings, starting in February 1968. The men expressed the need for a production bonus to stimulate the group to co-operate. Managment worked out a suggestion, which was presented in May. However, progress slowed down about that time, because the broader aims of the project tended to be displaced and *reduced* to a 'discussion about compensation to operators for running the department without foremen'. At this point the researchers were consulted. In order to redirect attention to the broader perspectives, they suggested that representatives of management and operators should visit Norsk Hydro's fertilizer plant at Herøya, which at that time was making very good progress in their own project, also part of the same ID Action Research Program. Representatives from Norsk Hydro later participated in a meeting for operators at Hunsfos. Together these exchanges of experiences helped to bring the PM 3-4 project back on track, and was also useful to the Hydro people.

Before summer 1968 the parties concerned agreed on a six-months 'experiment' to include a temporary 'sheltering' of the experimental area, and the introduction of a new payment system. The latter included a production bonus with emphasis on paper quality and compensations for multi-job training, for participating in theory courses and for operating without foremen. This arrangement was accepted by the men by *a vote of 34 to 15.*

During summer vacations, usually a difficult period, two of the shifts operated without foremen, and from September all the shifts began autonomous functioning, without shift foremen. Regular morning meetings with participants from management, the Action Committee and four to five operators were introduced. This facilitated communications and encouraged the men to bring up a long list of suggestions for improvements. Management also used the morning meetings to provide information about the economic situation, prices on raw materials and paper, production statistics, machine-hour costs, the market situation and company policy.

In the autumn the men improved their co-operation along the various steps in production (i.e. the beaters, the papermachines and the winders), and productivity and attitudes of participants towards the project were satisfactory. However, two sets of problems arose. The first set included the not surprising difficulty for a single operator representative in the Action Committee to keep sufficiently in touch with his 50 fellow workers on four shifts. The men also expressed a need to 'see more of their managers' and required that management should respond more rapidly to the various suggestions that were brought up.

The second set of problems concerned negotiations about workforce reductions throughout the company announced by management in October. Even though there would be no lay offs, reductions in manning are always unpleasant. However, the PM 3-4 people decided not to let this influence their project; and in fact they managed to negotiate a better solution than those being achieved in the other departments which had to go through arbitration to reach their agreements. Arbitration has often been used as a way of conflict resolution at Hunsfos.

By December 1968, at the end of the initial project period, the operators decided, by a *vote of 35 to 3*, that the project agreement should be prolonged by a further six months.[6] At this point the Action Committee was dissolved and the Department Committee, which included one operator representative from each shift, took over responsibility for the project, allowing each shift team to develop its own way of working. Hence, it was decided to let the men that had previously been appointed safety representatives to look after the project development as well. This did not turn out to be the best solution, and in the spring of 1969, the union representatives urged that weekly shift meetings with management should be held in the PM 3-4 Information Centre. They also demanded that minutes from the meetings should be taken in order to improve communications, across shifts in particular.

Yet it is illustrative of the competence and flexibility developed by the PM 3-4 teams that, in 1969, they were the only one of the continuous process departments that carried out the summer holiday schedule in four '2-week

6. The total number of votes is smaller than before, because of reduced manning levels.

periods' instead of five. At this point a high level of satisfaction among the operators including satisfaction with the bonus payments[7] was reported. The men also suggested to go ahead and further improve the pay system in PM 3-4 by making it more like a salary system with reduced pay-differentials among individuals, but this was rejected by the annual union meeting. The meeting demanded that in this matter all departments would have to be considered at the same time. The union insisted that from now on shift representatives be elected by the shift itself, and that criteria of selection be more adequate to project requirements.

In the autumn of 1970 the PM 3-4 project had evolved to a stage where the formal hierarchy which included production engineer, superintendent and day foreman could be replaced by a 'management team' which included the production engineer and a new 'production assistant' position (previously the day foreman), both working direct with the shift operator groups. Thereby, lines of communication became shorter and the contact area between management and men became broader and more direct.

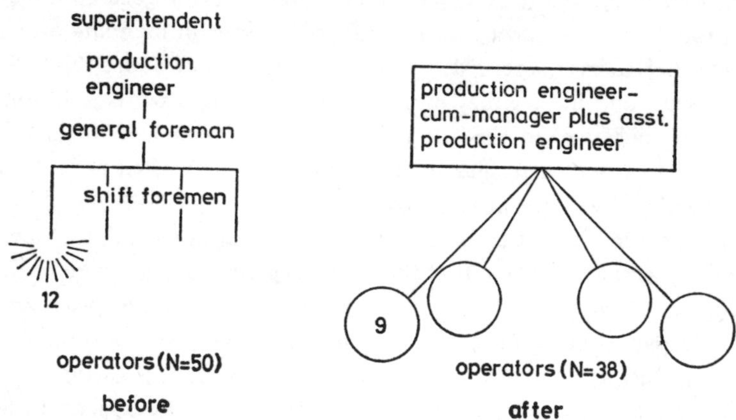

In contrast to the experiment in the CPD, the PM 3-4 management and operators through their Action Committee carried the initiative right from the beginning, using outsiders (the CPD Action Committee, the representatives from Norsk Hydro and the researchers) only when they themselves felt the need for it. Still it was the ideas embodied in the CPD experiment, which made possible the breakthrough at Hunsfos in 1967 by convincing both the management and the union that *the ID-project line of organizational redesign* might be worthwhile to pursue.

7. At this point the production bonus for all departments had already been changed to encourage the men to improve paper *quality* and reduce waste.

5. The Electric Panel Department

5.1. Preparation for experiment

The NOBØ Factories had been selected by the Joint Research Committee to become the first experimental site in 1963. However, the management of the company felt at that time that the risk of this project being caught up in political struggles was too great and asked to be relieved of the task as an experimental site. In 1965 management came back to the research team and proposed that the company start a project in a department for electrical panel heaters that had recently been opened in a small plant outside the main company location. The company had grown rapidly during the last few years, particularly since 1960 when export started to increase substantially. Sales almost doubled from 1960 to 1964 when they reached $ 6,000,000 almost half of this due to export.

The company itself was in metal sheet fabrication and hence was labour intensive with a strong tradition of workstudy and piece rates. Office furniture had become a main item of production as have electric panel heaters and traditional radiators. In the five previous years it had doubled its sales with almost half being exported.

The experimental plant was situated in Hommelvik, a small community 15 miles outside Trondheim, where NOBØ bought old premises for production which did not fit into the main plant. Approximately 75 workers were employed here under the direction of a production engineer in close co-operation with the main office. About 30 of these were employed in the experimental department. There were no foremen but 'contact men' had been appointed within each major production area. They would report to the engineer when something had to be corrected to keep the work flowing. Specialists from the main plant could be called upon but usually problems were simple and were solved on the local level. Sales, purchase of raw materials and product specifications were handled by the main plant. Recruitment of workers was left to the local manager. Until 1965 there had been considerable production fluctuation in the Hommelvik plant because the main factory usually placed there the small odd lot orders. In 1965 the manufacture of electric panel heaters was started on a new production line similar to a previous one in the main factory. This new line gave the Hommelvik department a stable production base and other products assumed a secondary role.

The initiation of the research project on the shop floor was rather informal. The production manager had told the local production engineer and the chief shop steward that NOBØ would like to start an experiment and preliminary agreement was reached. When the research team came to the plant to explain the conditions for carrying out the experiment, no one had any objections. The first phase would consist of a socio-technical study of the department. We stressed that the project was part of a national research and development program but it was not easy for people on the plant level to see the relevance of this. The first two field experiments had taken place in very different kinds of production and the general principles of job design were not easy to explain since local examples could not be discussed concretely. The production manager expressed the hope that local initiative could now be exercised in co-operation with the research team. The existing production line had been established according to the principles followed in the main plant; people had been trained for specialised jobs and had reached a normal level on individual piece rates (mainly based on MTM). Now it was up to the project to prove that other methods were better. We would have full freedom in organisational matters as long as we kept within the general agreements and were able to have the products produced according to specifications and delivery time without increasing costs.

In a formal meeting with all the workers involved we explained the basic idea of how we thought the conditions for greater participation could be improved. We referred to the results in the first experiment and stressed that the project would not commit the parties involved for more than one phase at a time. No basic objections were raised and the general attitude was positive, although no active participation occurred except from the shop steward committee which seemed to have the full confidence of the workers.

The layout and main tasks of the experimental department were split up in three main production groups. The panel heaters went through three stages:

Stage 1: mechanical operations of pressing, welding and grinding.
Stage 2: Surface treatment; cleaning, spray-painting and drying.
Stage 3: Assembly work along the main line with adjoining sub-assemblies and a packing operation at the end.

Most of the assembly work is of a simple character and takes place along tables where operators lift or push a small batch of semi-finished products from one work station to the next. Working conditions are rather pleasant for a workshop in an old building (apart from stage 2, where fumes from spray painting may cause some discomfort). There was a lack of storage space in the department, which sometimes hindered the flow of work between and within the three main phases of production.

Major characteristics of the technical system which we had to consider were as follows:

1. The entire production cycle was geographically and functionally separated from other organisational units.
2. The inputs of raw materials, product specifications, technical services and know-how were stable because of the links to the major factory. The output variations in terms of quality and quantity were easy to observe, and we were informed that the only critical factor would be to meet the quantitative demands of a market which would absorb everything the department could produce. (We questioned this information and were assured we should not worry about it, but sales turned out not to be as simple as that.)
3. The step-by-step transformations along the production line were easily observable and the information necessary to regulate the production was evident in the process itself.
4. The production line was split up in simple, specialised and repetitive jobs designed by traditional work studies and Method Time Measurements, (which formed the basis for individual wage incentives).
5. Explicit scheduling of batches was needed to co-ordinate operator and machine capacity.
6. The critical production variable was the speed of manual operations. Some co-ordination was required to cope with minor technical breakdowns or other bottlenecks that might appear along the line. There was very little quality dependence between jobs. Statistical quality control took place at the output end, for the product as a whole. The sequence of operational units was set by the product design, layout and assembly plan.

Major characteristics of the social system. Twenty-seven operators were working in the department when the project started (15 more were added during the next two months). Half of the men had industrial experience whilst most of the female operators were girls on their first industrial job.

About one third of the female operators were housewives (average age 38) who had taken the job to add to the family income.

The social stratification was reflected in the base rate paid. Young girls (under 18) were paid kr. 2.86 (40 cents) an hour while male workers (with 8 years of experience) were paid kr.5.37 (75 cents). Piece rates, on the average 60% of base rate, came on top of this.

The social system was structured around the production engineer (local manager) in his office and a number of working areas, each with a 'contact man' or charge hand. Contacts with the outside world were handled through the company headquarters and the engineer's main task when the project started was to co-ordinate the work flow inside the plant. He was assisted by a clerical worker and two men who helped the women on the shop floor and supervised their work. In most work groups an experienced man had an informal leading hand role.

The task structure along the production line was rigid except for variations in the speed of the manual operators. No social interaction between work roles was presupposed except contacts through the 'charge hands' to the engineer who would then take the necessary precautions to re-establish balance of the system when something unusual had occurred. This frequently occurred.

The general attitude of the workers towards the company was positive. They found the work easy, though often boring. Their lack of experience of other industrial settings made it difficult to get comparative data on worker satisfaction. Management considered the operators very co-operative, dependable and easy to deal with, something that was ascribed to the high quality of people living in this rural community.

5.2. Experimental program

Recommendations for experimental change were directed towards overcoming the one basic shortcoming of the work organisation viewed as a sociotechnical system i.e. the rigidity and segmentation of the social system that made it difficult to cope with the variations in human and task requirements. It was further proposed that joint optimisation of the social and technical system was more likely to be achieved if flexibility were sought by application of the general psychological criteria of job design, outlined in the first part of this report.

Three partly autonomous work groups were planned, each covering one of the main phases of production. Job rotation within each group, and to some extent between groups, was to take place according to the common objective, to achieve a daily target number of electric panels.

On the basis of these main principles the specific conditions of the experiment were spelled out and agreed upon by the end of 1965. The main points were:

1. Retraining of the operators to cope with more than one job and to adjust to variations in work loads by their own reallocation of tasks.
2. Training of 'contact persons' in each of the three groups who would co-ordinate variations between groups and plan production in consultation with group members.
3. Establishment of a departmental production bonus calculated on the number of panels produced per day.
4. A system of control and feedback of results in quantitative and qualitative terms.
5. The responsibility of the work groups in relation to the production engineer was clarified, the latter to concentrate on the plant's inputs and outputs. The work groups were to exercise responsibility for co-ordination and control within and between the work groups.
6. Some degree of decentralisation in maintenance would take place and some minor technical changes to facilitate the group system of work.

The first phase of the experiment lasted 3 months from December 1965. The experimental conditions were established in the following way:

1. The operators were trained in a two week program to cope with two to five jobs.

2. The election and training of contact men at first seemed simple enough since there were already people in the department who had filled similar jobs. However, the new role required a much higher degree of joint problem solving and personal participation. The female workers left most of the decision making to the men, something which was in line with the old work culture but in conflict with conditions for autonomous group functions.

3. The departmental production bonus was easy to establish for groups 1 and 3. The old piece rate system was used as a basis for the new bonus which would be calculated on the total number of panels produced per hour.

A guarantee was given that a flat rate, 55% on the old piece rate basis, would be paid during the experiment, if results did not get up to this level of production. For the surface treatment agreement could not be reached on the same basis, since there had been some unsettled questions regarding the equipment and other technical details previous to the experiment. This group had to be excluded from the experiment in the following two phases.

4. Feedback of results was technically easy to arrange although it turned out that no one in the department had a full understanding of the details of quality control, although it was the same as before. Once the reasons for sending back batches of unacceptable panels were discussed, there were no more problems with quality. The major problem was that almost none of the young female workers was interested in the production results (see point (2)). They continued to control their work pace and limited their co-operation to a level which they calculated to produce the same as the old 60% piece rate earning. During this phase the productivity was only slightly above the level agreed upon as the base line for the experiment.

In several group discussions questions were raised such as: 'Do they produce as much as we do?' In one meeting one of the older women claimed that she felt that the group system was unfair to those who worked hardest and she had never really accepted the new system. A split between the young girls on the one side and the rest of the workers on the other seemed difficult to bridge.

5. One major problem occurred which made it impossible for the production engineer to stabilise the boundary conditions of the department. Excessive seasonal variations in the market hit the department and two alternatives, both unfavourable, confronted the experiment. Production could continue as before and increase the unsold production to the point necessitating full close-down of the department in the post-experimental period. (The workers would work themselves out of a job.) The alternative was to arrange a gradual decrease in production and transfer operators to other in-plant jobs. This was done, and resulted in a considerable loss of group spirit. Co-ordination and planning became more difficult and a number of ad hoc arrangements were necessary.

It also turned out that the production engineer did not find it easy to leave the groups to make their own decisions or to take a firm stand with the main office of the company. Several discussions took place in which he had to defend himself against claims from his boss and the local shop steward that he did not exercise the leadership expected of him. The active role of the research workers in the first phase of the project made it more difficult for him to change his role to a more active one when the real experiment took place.

The second phase of the experiment lasted the two months to May 1966. A number of group discussions took place to clarify the new system, particularly the role of the contact men. Slowly the conditions for self-regulation inside the groups were created. The group concept was understood in concrete terms related to tasks, communication and co-ordination. Self-management took on meaning as a way of handling a job and simultaneously giving social support and personal freedom within the restrictions of the task.

One dramatic event made clear what the autonomy of the group meant and how co-ordination between groups was dependent on planning. A brief planning session took place each morning. The sessions lasted about ten minutes. Previously about 45 minutes were lost at the end of the day in trying to get the figures for shift production settled. When several complaints came from the female operators regarding the planning done by the 'contact men', these men stepped out of their special role. The women were to take over the planning. Chaos occurred since none of them were trained for the task. Agreement was reached that the contact men would resume their role and the female operators unanimously declared their willingness to accept the agreement reached in the planning sessions.

When the latent conflicts between the sexes had come out in the open, the work roles seemed to fall into place, production and group spirit seemed to grow. The level of productivity was still limited to the 'magic 60%'. The passivity of the female operators continued to be a problem in relation to the objectives of the project, namely to increase the level of participation in decision making. However, attitudes toward the new system changed. The common opinion was that 'everything now moves smoothly'. There was agreement that conditions now enabled the groups to start the real experiment. (A preliminary attempt had been made to aim at a 65% level instead of the old 58% base line.) The next week the contact men forgot to correct for some absenteeism by dropping the group target and a level of 80% was reached.[8] After this the operators finally dropped the idea of the old

8. It was a similar occurrence of absenteeism that broke the ice in the CS experiment.

60% level and started to discuss how many panels could be produced under the existing conditions. The flexibility in the group was increased by job rotation. A check was made for one week and on the average 2.7 different jobs per shift were performed by female operators and 4.2 jobs by men.

A controlled experimental phase lasted for 10 weeks until the summer vacation 1966.

1. Two classes of work roles seemed to develop during this phase in spite of the attempt made by the research worker to even out the differences. The continued reluctance of the female operators to take an active role in the planning led them to restrict themselves to jobs on the machines or to assembly work. They made the automatic adjustments needed between adjoining work stations but little more. The men did the other jobs. They took on the more difficult and heavy operations and most of the co-ordinating tasks. According to previous experience we expected the groups to differentiate to a certain extent on the basis of difference in competence as the men had more seniority and more experience in the plant. But in this case, we could see that the culturally defined sex roles had a very clear added impact upon the differentiation of work roles.

2. The flexibility achieved by job rotation seemed to stabilise at a level adequate to cope with the technical and social variations. On the average, the workers now alternated between four main jobs in a week and two jobs in a day.

3. Satisfaction with the group system increased during this phase. Those who had been positive before remained so, and those who had been ambivalent or negative changed. The common answer when asked about the new system was that it was fine and that no one wanted to go back to the old system. The few who had some reservations mentioned that group work depended on who was in your group. They expressed the belief that under the old system the individual could decide how much he wanted to do. (This in fact had not been so.)

Absenteeism was significantly lower in the experimental department than for the plant as a whole. It seemed to have increased from 4.7% to 6.5% from the second to third phase but this was against the 10% average for all female workers in the plant. No variation in absenteeism occurred among men.

The fact that the surface treatment group had not come into the experiment was a problem for the department. Two groups, one before and one after the surface treatment, had to co-ordinate their tasks without the advantage of having the middle group involved in the common action program. This did not cause major problems but it was a source of constant irritation and perhaps some doubt still existed as to the seriousness of the whole exercise. The girls in the assembly constantly complained about the quality of the surface treatment. The surface treaters complained that they were constantly needled by the girls in the assembly group.[9] The chief shop steward pointed out to the research team that if the conditions for the third group to enter the experiment could not be settled, the superiority of the group system could not be considered proven.

Reduction of manning also caused considerable difficulties during the experiment because transfer to other jobs was hard on those who had to move. The remaining operators ran the risk that they would be left with the people who had the least ability to rotate between jobs. When the formal experiment ended before summer vacation 1966 only 4 men and 14 women were left in the experimental group.

Their final judgement on their degree of job satisfaction can be classified follows:

Table V.1.

Satisfied in jobs	Total
a. Interesting and adequate variation	7
b. Not very interesting, but adequate variation	5
c. Job too monotonous	3
d. The job is alright but dreary and monotonous	2
e. Dislike job; dreary and monotonous	1
	18

Follow-up studies were made at the end of 1967 when the group system had been operating for a year in the whole of the Hommelvik. Only 68 of the 73 workers could be interviewed. All had been with the plant through 1967 but some felt they had too little experience of prior working conditions to make a judgement. Their stated attitudes are summarised in the following table.

9. As appeared to be the dilemma of the boiler men in the Hunsfos experiment.

Table V. 2. Perception of job changes (per cent of 68 workers).

	Better now	Could not judge %	No change	Worse
Responsibility taken	77	4	19	0 = 100%
Participation in decisions	64	3	33	0
Learning on the job	47	13	34	6
Variety in the work	55	20	22	3
Mutual support on job	67	23	6	4
Meaningfulness of job	51	7	42	0
Relations to Management	60	32	4	4

A major breakthrough is reflected in these figures. When work resumed after the summer break in 1966 the women had dropped the traditional role and had played an active part. Maybe they had privately discussed their experiences over the summer break? We do not know.

Performance data for the changes in working methods showed that during the three experimental phases productivity (acceptable panels/man hours) steadily increased to give an overall 20% improvement; average bonus increased 11%.

In the twelve months of 1967 the whole Hommelvik plant showed a further 10% improvement in productivity over the last experimental phase. This productivity was considerably higher than the traditionally organised panel line in the main plant, and the cost lower. Bonus rose a further 13% during 1967.

The company management were well experienced in making these sorts of measures of worker productivity and well aware of the sorts of allowances that have to be made, often intuitively, for the effects of equipment change. They believed the observed changes were real and were significant. Their calculations also led them to believe that quality standards had improved and maintenance costs dropped.

Follow up studies in 1969 and 1970 showed further development of the group system. Thirteen service workers were integrated in five autonomous work groups and they started to share the production bonus. Productivity had continued to increase and earnings correspondingly. A change in the payment system was introduced to reflect the broader involvement by the workers in planning, service work, co-ordination etc. The variable part of payment was reduced from 40% to less than 5% and was based on a 3-monthly production plan and a wage agreement with built in productivity forecasts. In this way the planning perspective of the workers was increased to 3 months as against one day when they worked on individual piece rates.

Diffusion of the new principles of work organisation from the experimental plant to the main company did not take place. There the traditional production system was maintained. The management argument was that the workers were not really interested and that the old system gave better management control. Individual piece rates were assumed to be necessary to keep up productivity. In retrospect one can easily see that what was really at stake was management's basic ideas of work organisation.

When market demands increased the company decided to transfer all production of electric panel heaters to a new and much larger plant 20 km. away from the experimental one. Planning had gone on for some time before the workers of the experimental plant were properly informed. A confrontation took place and from then on the workers were really involved in planning the new plant. The majority of them agreed to join the new plant on the condition that the group system was used there. This condition was not readily agreed to. The new plant has however operated on the group manning principle for four years and has now grown to 400 workers.

6. The Norsk Hydro Fertilizer Plant*

The initiative for this experiment arose from the Norsk Hydro Company. This is one of Norway's largest companies with over 8,000 employees in the four production complexes it directly manages at widely separated sites around the country. As a science based industry – electro-chemical and petro-chemical – it has long prided itself on being a progressive influence on the Norwegian scene. A new president was appointed at the beginning of 1967. He quickly started discussions with the Heroya Workers Union, at the main complex, with a view to thrashing out a new approach to productivity. The sort of thinking that was brought into these discussions can be illustrated by a statement of the President's in 1968:

'A tremendous and world wide increase in knowledge has created a new foundation for the use of knowledge and ability in solving the problems of society and production.

Many people say that modern development in technology puts man out of function. This is not true. The individual will not lose his importance.

In industry the requirements of individuals increase. They must increase their competence and initiative, and the value of machinery, raw materials and processes which the individual person is given responsibility for, is steadily increasing. More than ever before the crucial matter behind the progress in society, in industry and for the individual person is to make proper use of man's abilities and initiative.'

On the same occasion two of the leading shop stewards Tor Halvorsen and Arne Johnny Hansen wrote, on behalf of their Union (HAF):

'The idea of participation represents nothing new in HAF. For a long time we have understood that we must participate in order to obtain great results within industry. The best results are never reached after a one-sided evaluation. Today all positive forces must be released in a constructive participation. Today only the best results are good enough.'

Independently of, but parallel to, these discussions the management and shop stewards met representatives from the Hunsfos plant in a national

* This chapter is based mainly on follow up reports by Gulowsen (1974).

labour-management seminar and discussed in concrete terms the experiences from that experiment. With the agreement of the Joint Research Committee the management decided that the company would start up its own experimental studies and itself finance whatever assistance it needed from the research team.

As the first experimental site the company chose a new fertilizer plant being constructed at Heröya. This offered the very great advantage of not having to first overcome an established managment system and old customs and practices. It had the further advantage that the existing fertilizer plant, which was alongside it, would provide some basis for comparing performance. The overall purposes of the experiment were to be the same as for the earlier experiments. Increased productivity was not expressed as an aim in itself, but it was stated that the project could not be accepted if it ran contrary to the normal long term development of productivity.

6.1. The Action Committee

From the start it was clear that the experiment should proceed via the active collaboration of management and the local union. A declaration of the project was drawn up and signed by both these parties. An important clause in the bulletin they issued was that which gave protection to the experimental area:

> 'If it is convenient or necessary to change the organisation, the division of functions or the payment system from the usual pattern within the company, this may be done within the experimental area provided such changes are granted to have no immediate consequences outside the experimental area.'

Of course the agreement did not allow a completely free hand. The overriding constraint was that the experiment should come up with forms of participation that would be economically viable in fertilizer production *and* acting as a demonstration model foı the rest of the company. Getting an experimental success by extending special advantages to the workers in the experiment was thus not an acceptable solution.

To carry through the agreement an action committee was decided upon. Drawing upon the experiences of the earlier experiments it was felt that such a special body would be needed to help the change process and to cope with the temporary load on communication channels that the experiment would create. The specific needs that were identified were:

1. contact with the local management and authority within the area.
2. contact with the workers to secure their confidence
3. drawing upon technical competence in the fertilizer production
4. contact with the personnel department in order to secure information from within the company as well as to make a future diffusion easier
5. contact with the research workers

To meet these needs the following people were appointed to the action committee:

The head of the fertilizer department (chairman)
One representative from the local trade union
A charge-hand from the old factory
A representative from central management
A representative from the local personnel department
A representative from the Work Research Institute

The last mentioned provided the ongoing link to the resources of the research team.

As it turned out the action committee was not the prime source of the new job design but it did carry out most of the preliminary reality testing of the ideas. In all its other functions the committee proved invaluable. Two of its members were continuously present in the fertilizer plants. They maintained effective two-way communication so that many of the misunderstandings and difficulties that plagued some of the earlier experiments were dealt with before they started trouble. They not only kept the committee aware of the atmosphere in the plants but were able to feed in ideas, observations and suggestions from the operators and supervisors.

The action committee launched the project by organising a meeting which was attended by nearly 100 per cent of all employees in the old fertilizer plant (recruitment for the new plant had not yet begun). At this meeting committee members outlined the objectives of the experiment and the ideas behind it. The interest displayed and quality of the discussion directly reflected the high morale of the plant. As the men themselves were anxious to point out there had been important steps towards participative management in the preceding year. So they felt they knew what the experiment was driving at and, from their own experience, they knew that this was a way to get a good co-operative atmosphere and better production. The contrast with the first meeting of the wire drawing experiment could hardly have been greater.

Following the mass meeting the action committee moved to protect the experiment from outside influences that would have reduced the range of experimental choice. With the support of the operators they prevailed upon the plant manager to postpone, and eventually cancel, a manpower study that an external consulting firm was supposed to carry out and also to postpone the introduction of UMS. (UMS is a standard time system for planning and paying maintenance work.)

As the experiment took shape the action committee became increasingly immersed in the urgent task of recruitment, training and the wage system. We will return to this after dealing with the critical phase – the emergence of a design for operating the new fertilizer plant.

6.2. Design proposals

Although the new plant had a vastly improved layout and included some important technical innovations both plants were largely automatic, heavily instrumented and equipped with centralised controls. The sheer volume of dry and liquid materials being transported through the many stages of production meant a high but variable load of maintenance work and constant monitoring at many points.

The operators have little manual work, but must move across large areas which can include many physical levels. At intervals they visit one of the control rooms which are natural centres of communication. It is characteristic for this kind of process technology that work is fairly relaxed when the production is high and stable. The workers are only kept busy performing a limited number of routine tasks. However, work becomes very hectic when production starts to go out of control.

For an outsider the dimensions of the factory make a great impression. Many will also be struck by the fact that one can go through large parts of the factory without meeting anyone.

Process flow, layout and the information system create natural divisions in the factories. Each of the units has a separate control room and is manned with up to five operators. Both factories have their own small mechanical workshops, which can handle the majority of the day-to-day maintenance tasks.

The old factory consisted of two geographically separated areas and the workers were divided into two sub-groups. Each of these sub-groups was supervised by a charge-hand who acted as trouble-shooter. The charge-hands reported to the shift foreman.

Most of the maintenance was done by a local maintenance group which reported to the department management. However, breakdowns which had to be corrected on night shifts were handled by a shift pool of maintenance workers. These people did not report to the department management. A low status group of day workers did the necessary cleaning and labouring.

At an early stage in the construction of the new factory, in fact many months before the new approach was started, an experienced production engineer had designed the organization and manning scales for operating the plant. His ideas were based on the traditional methods of work organisation and on the technological specifications of the new factory. Although his ideas were never put into practice, we will examine his model since it shows the way many engineers in that and many other companies thought and still think about work organisation.

The engineer's original model included the following proposals. Every shift should be under the supervision of a foreman, who would be in charge of the whole factory. Technical specifications suggested that the factory could logically be divided into three areas, therefore the shift group should also be divided into three corresponding sub-groups, each of them under the supervision of a charge-hand. The operators within each group would be allocated three different skills grades with the charge-hands on the highest level. Two highly skilled operators would be in charge of the central control room. A special day force reporting to a day foreman would be responsible for cleaning, labouring and transport activities. Maintenance would be organised as in the old factory.

When the participation experiment commenced in March 1967, the total research group, with Professor Louis Davis, visited and studied the old factory and the plans for the new one. This group interviewed many of the people in the department, collected data and made a socio-technical analysis.

A meeting between representatives from management, supervisors, the workers in the department and the social scientists, produced another organisational model that was suitable for both factories.

This model was based amongst other things, on an analysis of the maintenance data from the old factory. This data suggested that various kinds of repair work were significant parts of the daily work load throughout the the factory. In fact, it proved to be difficult to separate maintenance from normal process operations. Since the new factory appeared to be divided into a number of separate geographical units, it was suggested that each shift should consist of sub groups structured in the following way.

Each sub-group should include at least one worker who possessed versatile maintenance skills. The idea was that each sub-group should possess the skills and the working capacity necessary to tackle most of the production variances that occurred in their area. The model did not include chargehands as this was not seen as necessary. The basic idea of the model was to provide conditions for increased self sufficiency and autonomy at group level and better opportunities for learning and work satisfaction for individual group members.

The different implications of the two approaches can be readily seen in following manning tables.

Table VI. 1. Manning levels for the new plant.

Initial proposal based on classic scientific management principles (1967)		Subsequent proposal based on semi-autonomous groups (1967)
Plant manager	1	1
Production assistants (clerks)	2	2
Superintendent	1	1
Day foreman	1	0
Shift foreman	4	4
Maintenance foreman	1	1
Shift charge-hands	12	0
Shift-operators (12 × 4)	48	40
Maintenance workers	12	8
Day labourers	12	0
Total	94	57

This reduction of forty per cent needs to be closely examined as it highlights the differences in organisational principles. The reduction had nothing to do with lowering the targets for level of plant efficiency nor with burdening the workers: the management would not allow the first and the unions would certainly not allow the latter. It comes from a difference in principle. In the first design an over-riding principle was that every necessary task had to be identified as the responsibility of a particular individual. The individual was then pinned to the geographical area where 'his tasks' were located. His own specified work load had to be so gauged that he could be expected to cope with 'normal peak load'. In this plant it was easy to calculate, from the performance data of the old plant, that most of the operators would have nothing to do but watch a great deal of the time, even though their neighbours might be experiencing a temporary overload. The shift charge-hands provided a floating reserve of multi-skilled men. They and the foremen could temporarily reallocate duties to help with crises but even this was limited by the fact that each individual tends to know only his own jobs. The next level of back-up was provided by the maintenance staff and the day labouring gang. These people took the load of these kind of tasks off the operators and theoretically allowed for maximum utilisation of operators on operating tasks.

We started, as on the earlier experiments, from the principle of group responsibility for as much as possible of the necessary tasks in their area. It would be up to the group to deploy and re-deploy themselves so as to cope with variations in task loads and still ensure adequate monitoring over the processes still running in control. To effectively operate in this way the members of the group would need to be multi-skilled to the point where they could at least lend a hand with any of the tasks coming up in their area (as were the charge-hands in the previous design). Because of the sheer physical size of the plant it was recognised that a shift would normally operate as three small sub-groups. On our calculations it seemed that a shift crew of ten could be sufficiently flexible to cope with the operating tasks *and* with many of the less skilled maintenance tasks, *and* with all of the cleaning and moving tasks. The management and union representatives accepted the desirability of the shift crew coping with these other tasks. Too much down-time was due to waiting for the maintenance men or from someone failing to use a spanner before trouble actually occurred. Similarly, spillage was not unrelated to the operators' carefulness and alertness. However, both parties felt it would be prudent to set shift manning at *eleven*. They also felt that it might be difficult to recruit up to two skilled maintenance men per shift to work in the teams as operator-maintenance men. (They were right. The plant finished up with only one per shift.)

It was expected with the new system that the shift foremen would for the most part be acting-in for the manager and superintendent, not acting as a supervisor and of course he would not have a set of charge-hands to organise.

One final feature of the design should be noted. Everyone on shift could expect to be skilled up to the level of control room operation. An understanding of automated process plant operation requires a close and up-to-date view of things from the centre and from the floor level. Under the classic one man/one job approach control room operators tend to be wedded to their 'white collar job' and its attendant status, and such a two-way view of operations is stultified.

Thus instead of the traditional sort of status differences between unskilled day labourers, ordinary operators, control room operators and charge-hands there would, in our design, be only differences in currently proven competence. Achievement of higher competence was expected to be largely up to the individual. He would not have to wait until a vacancy occurred at the next level, when even then he may have had no prior chance to prove his fitness to compete for the vacancy.

6.3. Developments in the design

Two months after the meeting that considered these alternative designs one of the engineers in the division brought forward a 'new' proposal based on discussions within the local management group. These were:

1. Each process worker would be responsible for cleaning and labouring in his own work area.
2. There should be no low-skilled daytime groups in the factory.
3. Each shift should have a charge-hand in addition to the foreman. This charge-hand should have some competence in instrumentation and in addition be capable of acting as a troubleshooter for the whole factory.

This proposal accepted the suggestion that a day cleaning squad be avoided. In other ways, it was a rearguard action. The reversion to individual/task area responsibility and to charge-hands would have eliminated the notion of semi-autonomous groups. The 'job enlargment' entailed in each man having to do his own cleaning would probably not have been seen by the union as 'job enrichment'.

The Action Committee gradually came to their own conclusions regarding the design of the organisation. There should be no charge-hands and no low status day workers in the factory. Shift operators should be urged to work in pairs or in larger groups within their own group territory. The shifts should, if possible, be manned with some maintenance people. (The number of maintenance people who applied for jobs in the factory was limited. Thus each shift, which numbered about 12 operators, had only one or two maintenance workers when the factory started up.)

Using these ideas as their point of departure, the different shift groups subsequently developed their own ways of working the new organisational patterns. The major differences were in the degree of multi-skilling they were prepared to accept and the size of geographical areas they were prepared to man. The older workers showed less interest in increasing their skills and, not unnaturally, more interest in minimising walking and climbing stairs.

Before the shift groups did anything, or even came into existence, the action committee had a lot to do themselves, and a lot to work out with others, before the proposals for semi-autonomous group manning could become operational.

6.4. Wage system and bonus

It was obvious that the new manning proposals offered considerable economic advantages to the company, provided they worked. It was equally obvious that some new wage system would be needed to bring advantages to the operators and to go on doing so in the likely event of the new system continuing to create further advantages for the company.

The previous experiments gave some leads to the action committee, but not more. They were not seen as providing any model that could simply be copied. Before the committee could move an overall site productivity agreement was finally settled in April 1967. This agreement offered all the workers on the site, including the old fertilizer plant, an opportunity to earn more. This agreement included a manpower analysis which was to be taken care of by a consultant firm, and the introduction of piece rates for maintenance work according to a so-called Universal Maintenance System (UMS).

At a plenary meeting the workers in the fertilizer factory questioned the applicability of this productivity agreement to the project area. They saw the principles as irreconcilable because the manpower analysis started from the principle of one man – one unshared responsibility. They also questioned the competence of outside specialists.

With this background, the workers suggested that their own manpower analysis should be taken care of by the action committee. This was done in co-operation with the local management. The proposal which suggested a reduction in the manning of the old plant from 72 to 60 workers, was unanimously accepted. Later the maintenance group was reduced from 12 to 8 people.

The old fertilizer plant, after this event, followed more or less the same pattern as was developed by the new plant when it gradually started to operate on the new basis during the early autumn of 1967.

Next the action committee, aided by the local management, worked out a bonus scheme for all operators in the old fertilizer plant. This bonus was based on the following criteria:

1. Production volume of acceptable quality
2. Control over raw materials lost, particularly nitrogen
3. Other costs which could be influenced by the workers
4. Total number of man-hours for production, including service workers' time

The central idea behind the bonus scheme was to pay the workers according to factors which they themselves could influence; factors which at the same time were important for the factory. Since the bonus included all workers in the factory, it was expected to stimulate co-operation. The payment and the working conditions for each individual depended upon the joint effort of the whole factory staff; operators, maintenance, clerks and supervisors.

The bonus scheme represented the first step towards a new wage system for the new factory. It soon became clear that more drastic changes would become necessary.

The traditional wage system put people in a position where it was not in their interest to help each other and hence it acted against co-operation and mutual aid in the work situation. It did less than nothing to encourage a way of work that could provide opportunities for learning from each other, for sufficient variation, for the development of work groups and for the operators to get to know the whole process. In other words, chances for satisfaction of the psychological job requirements were small.

In order to improve the chances for satisfactory psychological work conditions, the action committee devised a new wage system. In close co-operation with the local shop stewards, it was decided that each man should be paid according to his proven competence. Both theoretical knowledge and practical experience from production could contribute to higher wages. By learning all the jobs in the factory, the process operators could advance from wage class no. 2 to class no. 6, and get then the same wage level as skilled maintenance workers. The wage system presupposed that the workers were given the chance to rotate through all jobs in the factory.

It was hoped that this would reward the workers for learning from their work and step-by-step developing more flexible interdependent work patterns. It was agreed that the local shop steward and the general foreman should be responsible for the evaluation of the competence of the workers. This wage system was to turn out as a major innovation. For management, it was a challenge. Would lower manning rates and better performance offset the added costs of training and paying extra for having a reserve of competence on the job?

6.5. Recruitment to the new factory

The workers who became superfluous through their own rationalisation in the old factory, were guaranteed jobs in the new plant. But it was necessary to recruit more people. A lot of discussion took place about how the vacant positions should be advertised. It was agreed that any such advertisement should create only those expectations that were in line with the intended design of work. The final advertisement was as follows:

'We need workers to take care of process and maintenance in the new fertilizer factory (process workers, maintenance workers, plumbers and instrument makers). The company is going to try to develop new kinds of co-operation to the benefit of employees as well as the company itself. Therefore, we want to get into contact with employees who are interested to:

1. learn and develop themselves further through the work
2. take responsibility
3. become active members of a work group
4. participate in the training of others
5. participate in developing jobs and ways of co-operation which create conditions for personal development through the work.

It may be necessary to alter many of the usual norms within the organisation, such as formal organisation and contents of the different jobs. At the moment, it seems likely that work groups with optimal competence within maintenance and process control will have to be formed.'

No financial incentive was mentioned. The advertisement generated more than enough applications. Selection was based on interviews by a representative from the personnel department, the general foreman of the factory and the trade union representative in the action committee. Concerning wages, the operators were assured that they would not lose anything compared to their old level whilst training till the new factory was started. No other guarantees were given.

This procedure differed significantly from established routines in the personnel department of the company. The 20 workers who were selected according to the procedure which has just been described, made up the first group to join the staff for the new factory. The majority of the remaining part of the staff came from the old factory and joined somewhat later. This group had not been through special selection.

6.6. Training

Traditionally process operators in Norsk Hydro, as in most other companies, have received little systematic training and education. They have generally had to prepare themselves for the performance of relatively simple routine tasks by working together with a more experienced worker. The narrow specialised jobs gave little opportunity to understand the process as a whole and did little to stimulate further learning. Only half of the 20 new men had even this much experience of process work. So the action committee immediately took the initiative to set up a training scheme. A course of 200 hours of theoretical training was started in co-operation with the company school and the local shop stewards. Practical experience and training went on in the old factory and later in the new factory as equipment was being installed.

Due to lack of time to commissioning date only the first group of workers went through the whole training program. The rest of the workers, all experienced men, were given a shorter theoretical training program lasting 40 hours.

The character of the training was dictated by the desire to man the factory with multi-skilled operators having a broad knowledge in process maintenance work. They were therefore provided with learning opportunities in chemistry, process knowledge, instrumentation and maintenance work.

The interest in the training program was great, and the operators constantly probed the connection between the theory and their future work. Supervisors and technicians on the factory staff participated in the course both as teachers and as students.

The training scheme, which was built up for the workers in the fertilizer department, represented a 'new deal' in the training policy within the company. Previously the company school had mainly been occupied by training craftsmen in craft skills: plumbers, welders and mechanics etc. The majority of those trainees were under 20.

The new training scheme was a first step towards creating in the company the status of a 'skilled process worker'. The need for adult training was stressed and new organisational and pedagogic principles were applied:

'The school must go into the factory; the factory must become the school' In particular it was believed that education for working as semi-autonomous groups should be based on semi-autonomous learning groups. As the pressure for multi-skilling built up on the site as a whole, there were signs of the education being routinised. We are in no position to judge whether the principle was ever firmly established in the company school or, if established, whether the observed tendencies remained central.

6.7. The operation of the new principles in the new plant

The critical test of the new principles of organisation was in this case quite simple. What was judged to be a good design by traditional 'scientific management' principles stated that about 94 people were needed if the plant were to be efficiently operated. The alternative design, based on self-managing multi-skilled shift teams, predicted that 56 people could operate the plant with at least equal efficiency and with greater satisfaction to the people concerned. The modified design went into operation with 60 people, one extra operator per shift. The difference in manning levels was still so great (60 to 94) that there could be no rational doubt that different principles were at stake. Differences in technology, personnel etc. were nowhere near comparable in magnitude of their possible effects on work satisfaction or efficiency.

The first two questions are thus:

1. Did the much lower manning level with semi-autonomous groups manage to achieve the level of efficiency that would be expected with a traditional design?
2. Did the workers benefit accordingly from the system (or was the per capita improvement in efficiency taken from their hides)?

Let us reply very briefly to the first question, turn to the second question, and then return to the first.

The new mode of operation was obviously economically viable by managements' standards. They encouraged the old fertilizer plant to move over to the same principles of operator self-management; they encouraged their other plants on the site to move in the same direction. Although this has been achieved only to a limited extent it is explicit company policy to push on in this direction. Over seven years of operation (1967-74) there has been no question of going back to the old principles of organisation. This managerial attitude was not due to Norsk Hydro having money to throw away, to sustained union pressure, or to public opinion. We will return to the question of what evidence could have been so convincing to management.

The most obvious and most easily measured advantages to the workers were those flowing from being multi-skilled, being able to increase their skills and being able to use and be paid for these additional skills. Less easy to measure, the advantages of themselves being able to make so many of the decisions about the deployment of their capabilities. Even less obvious, the advantages that accrue from disappearance of the donkey jobs of day labouring and the erosion of the 'labour aristocracy' of control room operators and charge-hands. (As welcomed and further pushed for by the paper machine operators at Hunsfoss).

The plant was commissioned in 1967. By late summer 1969 the average operator was being paid extra for competence in 5.4 out of the 8 possible task-skills in the plant. One shift lagged noticeably behind in multi-skilling and rotation of jobs and were also noticeably dependent on their shift foreman. These were older workers and this seemed to be their preferred style. In the overall pattern this was not disruptive. Observations made at this stage also showed that the average operator was involved in 2-4 different task areas during his shift. In the traditional system the operator was only rarely involved in more than his own one area and then had to be paid as if it were over-time (see Hunsfoss case). Multi-skilling was obviously the new norm. Even the 'laggard shift' had an average of above three skills. Flexibility in the use of these skills was markedly higher than in the old system and indicative of the new style of working.

Table VI.2. Changes in attitude of workers between previous job and December 1967 in the new plant.

		YES	NO
a. Do you have adequate responsibility for determining your work?	Old job	14	19
	New plant	24	1
b. Are there good chances to learn on the job?	Old job	10	21
	New plant	25	1
c. Is there adequate variety in the job?	Old job	16	17
	New plant	22	4
d. Does the job give you a sense of security?	Old job	13	20
	New plant	22	8
e. Do you feel satisfied with the job?	Old job	18	13
	New plant	26	0

A measure of the attitude of operators was taken after they had had some months of working the new system. Because of the work pressures in the factory only 33 of the 52 operators and maintenance men could be taken off the job to be interviewed at the start and only 22 in December 1972. Some of these respondents had worked in other equally traditional jobs but not in fertilizer production and others were in the maintenance section which was only marginally affected. The differences are striking enough to offset the inadequacies of the data.

Of critical significance is the fact that all but 1 worker on the new plant said that they could now determine how they did their jobs.

As social scientists we did not think it necessary to run statistical tests of significance over these figures; they were very obviously highly significant. After day-to-day experience of the new form of organisation for more than four months the workers thought they had more control, better chances to learn, more optimal variety, more satisfaction and more security.

Our systematic observations on the new plant continued through 1972. Some changes were occurring. The younger people with the higher levels of competence were expressing some dissatisfaction with lack of further challenge and applying (successfully) for new jobs in other parts of the company. The labour market, particularly within their own company was becoming very rosy. Thus whilst labour turnover was practically nil during the first two years, it is now more like that for operators in the other chemical plants on the site.

It is sometimes asked whether the effects we are describing here could not have been achieved by just making the same changes in wages and bonuses. It seems an appropriate point at which to confront such queries. Quite simply, what good would it have done the new plant to have paid for a high level of skill if this were used only within one individual's area of responsibility. What good would a group bonus have done if the men did not have the rights and responsibility of self-management? We suggest that self-management of the work groups is the key, not the lock to be turned by forms of monetary reward. This is rather obvious when we consider older forms of group working where money rewards sustained brutalised forms of sub-contracting within which employees had even less rights for self-determination and less legal protections against exploitation.

Self-management was not complete and was never intended to be so. However, there was no felt need nor any expressed desire for the return of charge-hands. In fact, when one foreman retired no one was formally appointed to replace him – one operator was informally asked whether he would look after the things the foreman used to do (answer outside phone and the like).

Observation of a typical shift cycle confirmed the 'de-centering' of the foreman on all but the one mentioned above.

Table VI.3. Persons consulted by operators about problems.

	Foreman	Other Operators	Both
Shift 3	7	2	0
Shifts, 1, 2, 4	8	11	4

Returning now to the company's apparent satisfaction with semi-autonomous group working. The most obvious fact is that the plant worked. It did not collapse from undermanning and it did not have to be kept on its feet by special support systems.

The evidence allows us to go beyond this simple statement of the key fact. The plant did not only work but it worked better than could have been expected on the traditional system of manning.

The bonus scheme was based on savings in inputs as well as increase in outputs. Adequate records of these were not brought into being until 1969 (the need for such data had not been recognised). In the two years 1969-70 the bonus increased about 50%.

Production data for each of the three main lines exist from commissioning time. They show increases between 50 and 100 per cent despite the low manning levels. The down-time percentage for the plant's operation was probably the most critical indicator. Down-time was the most costly experience the plant could have. It was expected from experience of this type of plant that down-time would vary between ten and thirty per cent (usually more than twenty per cent). In the new plant with the new form of organisation the down-time has been kept within five and ten per cent, much less than half. This was achieved by the increased concern of the operators, not by increased effort.

With the savings on inputs these reductions in down-time (with such low manning levels) might well explain the continued managerial interest.

6.8. Diffusion of project results on corporate level

Diffusion must be seen in the specific context agreed upon at the time the project was launched. It was Norsk Hydro, in collaboration with its related unions, which took the responsibility for the project and for evaluating the results. The joint national research committee agreed to the project plans in general and to the involvement of the research group.

When the new fertilizer plant had been in operation for a few months, the action committee presented a progress report to a joint meeting of company and union representatives. A decision was quickly made to start preparations for similar projects in other plants. Six months later the company magazine published the results from the fertilizer project and stated that the new principles of work organisation would constitute a shift in company policy. It soon became clear that this was easier said than done. One was obviously not dealing with an experiment and a simple transfer of results but with all the complexities of changing the largest private industrial organisation in Norway.

This occurred at a time when Norsk Hydro and its unions faced two serious challenges which diverted most of their resources away from the ID project. First, Norsk Hydro became a major partner in the North Sea Oil activities. Secondly, the national struggle over membership in the EEC made with a referendum deciding that Norway was not going to join. This caused considerable reorientation within the company, and its major union was divided politically to the extent that it could not mobilize its members in anything but traditional bargaining issues.

In view of these limitations, it is perhaps understandable that diffusion from the fertilizer project has been slow. One project in the carbide plant was just getting off the ground, after considerable resistance from the supervisor, when market conditions caused the plant to close down. An extensive project started in the magnesium plant which has included major technological improvements and retraining activities. Projects in a large mechanical workshop and in the transportation sector, were hung up on primitive bargaining of a new structure.

In 1970 a new wage agreement based on the model from the fertilizer project, was signed for the whole company, granting all workers the right to get training on the job and in special courses integrated in a guaranteed promotion ladder. A special incentive system (UMS) for maintenance workers, causing a split between process operators and special tradesmen, was gradually abolished. A two year program was set up to retrain 350 foremen for alternative supervisory roles (see Chapter 8). Most of them had had no formal education beyond the age of 15 and their average age was now above 50. In 1973 and 1974 a series of middle management seminars have been run to initiate small organisation redesign projects. Still no further real breakthroughs have occurred at the productive level to match the policy declarations of the company in 1968. Some of the reasons for this can perhaps best be understood if we explore on a more general level the trade union and management involvements in projects of this nature. We shall do so in the next two chapters.

Other reasons might have to be sought at our level. At Hunsfos, after a very difficult start-up at the chemical pulp plant, the machine operators on the paper machines took things very much into their own hands. They first worked out what they needed to do and then checked it out with the researchers, and with the operators at Porsgrun fertiliser plants. At the Heroya complex, despite the very successful start-up of the fertiliser plants, we implanted a resident expert. As if this were not enought to stifle local initiative the carbide plant experiment stopped because the market for carbide closed down. The magnesium plant experiment developed very slowly in the face of a massive technological re-design. The unions in the central workshops and in transportation would not consider re-design of jobs until they had settled outstanding scores with management, by arbitration.

We should perhaps at this stage have implemented the lessons of the Hunsfos paper mills. Namely, pulled out resident experts, and provided advice on-call. Our expertise might have just about become *the* block.

7. The role of the trade unions in the Industrial Democracy Project

7.1. The political background

The Trade Union Council in Norway is intertwined with the Labour Party and the political system. It has developed hand in hand with the Norwegian (social democratic) Labour Party since the 1920s. It came out of the depression in the early 30s, shaking off strong Comintern influence, with independent, industrial type unions (as distinct from the craft type unions). Its strength in the 1930s was the TUC protection from the centre, with each union free to bargain on behalf of the workers in each industry. At plant level a strong, but disciplined, shop steward system emerged. (There are no closed shops in Norway, but TUC affiliated unions normally organise approximately 70% of the workers in industrial plants, in large ones close to 100%.)

After 1935 no major economic or industrial policy had been put into effect by the Labour government without the consent and backing of the trade unions. When the government escaped from the German occupation in 1940 the TUC soon made a coalition with other major political and social organisations in underground Norway. A trade union leader, shot as a hostage by the Germans in 1941, became a symbol of the growing resistance. This helped to restore the unity of the labour movement and the political links between the exile government and the Home Front. Many TU leaders were in concentration camps or in the underground forces with politicians and young industrial managers who took leading positions in post-war Norway.

During the period of post-war reconstruction, the TUC was strongly involved in the Labour government's policy of imposing price and wage controls and productivity programs, until industry and the merchant navy were rebuilt. When the Labour Party dropped nationalisation as a general policy in the 1950s, the TUC supported the new centralized economic controls. These controls left the local shop stewards committees relatively free to work out their own solutions with their managements, within the framework of biannual contracts and the national guidelines for labour-management relations. Gradually the joint consultation system has been extended into new areas; of education and training, personnel administration and welfare, work organisation and production planning and control.

A trade union leader, Olav Bruvik, who later became minister of social affairs, was one of the first to recognise the need to renew the objectives of the welfare state. He insisted on the improvement of the quality of man's working life, not only in terms of job security and pay but also in terms of concrete conditions for participation in decision making in industrial organisations.

When Industrial Democracy became a political issue in 1960 it was the TUC which led the way to put the general ideas into concrete programs of action. In trying to do so the TUC found that it was up against a set of problems that no other trade union movement had been able to solve. *Apart from representative arrangements, what could be done with the actual work situation in industry to humanize work and increase the individual's control over his day-to-day work life*?

Joint consultation, backed by the TUC since World War Two, had contributed something to improving the communication between labour and management at the local level. However, it had not changed the organisation structure of firms; only to a limited degree had it improved personnel policy and management philosophy; and it had had very little impact on the participation of the great majority in the decisions affecting their daily work life.

The TUC was well aware of foreign experiences with workers control, co-determination etc. but was not tempted to copy models for Industrial Democracy from countries with different historical and social backgrounds. Usually, as in Yugoslavia, and West Germany, after the war, formal *representative* systems were the main content of Industrial Democracy. The Norwegian TUC did not underestimate this aspect, particularly in countries where trade unions were comparatively weak. But the TUC had no reason to underestimate its own strength in the well established representative system of labour-management bargaining and consultation in Norway. Its stated concern was with evolving *participative* democratic arrangements within industry.

7.2. The phase of initiation of the ID project

A number of conferences on industrial democracy had been held during 1960-61 by the TUC and the Labour Party, and social researchers from different institutes had been involved. In 1962, the TUC set up, with the Employers' Association, a joint national research committee on industrial democracy. This occurred after searching, informal consultations between TUC and industrial leaders on the one side and social scientists on the other.

There was a change of leadership in the TUC in the early 60s but not much working through of policy took place between the TUC and the individual national unions. In the joint research committee the particular historical background for ID in Norway was analysed. A conceptual clarification took place and a three-pronged action program emerged in the TUC One objective was to extend the areas of consultation and bargaining, and to strengthen the shop steward role at company level. A second objective was to experiment with new forms of work organization, and a third was to change the formal structure of company directorship, if necessary by law.

When the first phase of the ID project was completed in 1963 (including an empirical) study of employee representation on board level of companies) the national unions were not yet ready to tackle the policy issues of industrial democracy within their own union organisations. The unions were basically institutionalised to handle bargaining issues of a win-lose type, and simultaneously committed to support Labour Party policies. Wide TU acceptance of productivity programs after the war, including Tayloristic ideas of work organisation, made it difficult for national unions to engage in a research and development program to improve democratisation of the work place.

However, the TUC and the Iron Metal Workers' Union had no difficulty in opening up, for the research team, the first experimental field site, the wire drawing mill. The vice-president of the TUC had been a worker and chief shop steward in the same company. His support carried a lot of weight in the national union, and in the local union which organised all of the workers in the company. He was also trusted by the local TU shop stewards committee, the workers on the shop floor, and by the management of the company.

As reported in the presentation of the first field experiment the workers did not readily see the relevance of the ID project when we first entered the field site. However, the trust they had in the union and the open mind of the members of the shop stewards committee, gave us a chance, during a three months pilot study, to 'earn the right' to work in a collaborative relationship with people on the shop floor as well as the local union and management representatives.

We soon experienced that the clarification of objectives and ideas we had achieved at the level of the joint national committee had not come down the line of the TU structure. At no time before the end of the 1960s did the TUC set up a national campaign to involve some ten thousand people in discussions of 'everyday democracy'. In the national unions there was initially little real understanding of the two not necessarily complementary aspects of ID, namely; representative systems on the one hand and democratisation of the work place on the other. However, the value orientations of the shop stewards and their long experience in local problem-solving enabled them to quickly see the relevance of the field experiments in their plants. This then placed them on a higher level of involvement and commitment than generally existed in the headquarters of the national union. There was no lack of general acceptance of the TUC policy formulations and action programs. But these programs had not emerged from the expressed needs of those working at the grass root level of the trade unions. Furthermore, like most union headquarters they were understaffed and very much preoccupied with the main traditional tasks of the trade unions; organising members, collective bargaining and grievance handling. Considerable demands had also to be met for information and educational activities, for committee work and for routine administration.

During the first field experiment there were three events which served to test out the involvement and commitment of the local branch of the national union and the TUC.

1. *The introduction of the project at the shop floor*, its objectives and the principles to be observed by the research team, raised a number of problems which were all to be handled by the local shop stewards. How to protect the interests of workers who did not wish to participate? How to guarantee anonymity in the research reports of those who desired that? How to go from the experimental arrangement to negotiated agreements? How to share productivity increases? How to negotiate lower manning levels?

All these and similar questions were handled by the shop stewards rather efficiently. They checked with national headquarters when unusual contract matters came up. Only one issue needed further sanctioning by the union leadership. A regional union officer came down to a local meeting in the experimental department to explain the objectives of socio-technical experiments and the difference between these and productivity programs. After this meeting we were able to go ahead with the field experiment, but the national union had still not clearly realised that its post-war policy, favouring work study, individual incentive payments etc. would probably have to be revised if they were going to give real support to socio-technical experiments in industry.

Not everything at the shop floor could be handled by the shop stewards.

There are many local customs and feelings about job ownership that constitute a last line of defense. They are defended as such even against the union if the men feel they are threatened.

2. *Sanctioning of preliminary research reports* raised an important issue regarding the 'ownership' of the project. The research team had made it clear from the start that reports would have to be sanctioned both by representatives of management and local union, and distributed to those directly involved. This issue went straight from the field site to the top of the TUC. The vice-president of the TUC and the research team agreed that reports should be sanctioned jointly or simultaneously by management and union. Only in special cases where product specifications etc. had to be protected by the company would management have the right to insist on appropriate changes in the reports before further circulation took place. This solution was sanctioned by the next meeting of the joint national research committee. However, the policy problems involved for the national unions in sharing the responsibility for developmental experiments in industry had not then fully emerged.

3. *Evaluation of the research results* of the *first* experiment was a task in which we were not able to achieve a *joint* involvement by the local union and management. Management wanted separate meetings and the research team accepted this. Only too late did we understand that this was a tactical error. The shop steward committee went through the reports and gave their comments, but these were of a rather general character. Their real evaluation was demonstrated by their attempts to set up continued experiments on the basis of extended experimental conditions. These new conditions had to be accepted by management and when this did not occur continuation was blocked. We had failed to design a way in which the local union could themselves bring matters up to the national joint committee. Instead, the results were evaluated by the joint national committee in terms of their national

implications and they moved on to sanction new experiments in other industries.

The management of the first experimental company looked at the experiment as a simulated laboratory exercise which needed large scale replication before conclusions could be reached. At the same time management were startled by the novelty of the experiment in terms of the new solutions coming from the shop floor.

These three events illustrate an important aspect of Scandinavian trade unionism. The *local shop steward system* is capable of handling quite complicated policy matters at company level, even such matters which go beyond what is covered by traditional contracts. The TUC is also quite capable of taking a leadership role in such policy matters as Industrial Democracy, though usually in dialogue with the Labour Party. However, the *national industrial unions* are so preoccupied with traditional contract bargaining and administration that they have very limited ability to work out and channel policy matters from the individual work place up to the TUC, or from the TUC down the line.

7.3. The breakthrough in the second experiment

In the second field experiment there were several conditions in the initial phase which facilitated the strong role played by the union:

1. The admission of the research team to the plant was discussed jointly by management and two union representatives on the basis of introductory contacts from national headquarters. Informal information from the first experimental site was also available.
2. The chief shop steward was in a very strong position on the shop floor, in the company and in the local community. He very soon picked up some policy issues linked to specific problems, like the new role of supervision, job security in the face of technological change and market fluctuations and the impact of a new task structure on the system of payment.
3. The shop steward committee had intimate contacts to national headquarters and the president of the union visited the field site for critical meetings.

When the breakthrough came there had been confrontations between older workers in high status jobs and those in underprivileged jobs. There had also been confrontations between the experimental groups and three levels of management. In this way people knew what was at stake and who were on which side. The researchers had also been tested out and their roles were redefined in terms of acting as resource people for local task force groups. Their formal academic status had been reduced but their impartial positions were respected.

The breakthrough was characterised by the departmental action committee taking over the responsibility for further experimentation, under joint sponsorship and supervision of the top management and the shop steward committee. The researchers withdrew from their office at the field site and took the roles of outside resource people. The experimental conditions were partly within the range of contract negotiations (security, bonus etc.) partly within management responsibilities (production control, new equipment etc.) and partly within an area of policy making on branch level (new career and educational systems etc.). This forced policy matters on to management as well as the local union. After achieving a new plateau of performance and consolidating the field experiment the new forms of organisation were reinforced in explicit policies for joint consultation by management, the union and the labour-management bodies.

The second field experiment further demonstrated that the shop stewards and the local union branch could work out new policies for field experiments within the framework of the ID project. They were able to integrate the new principles of work organisation with their policies on job security, payment, status differentiation and vocational education. They backed management in new regional policies for employment and national educational policies. The local union got protection from national headquarters for their continued experimentation and influenced the national union in terms of educational policy and regarding systems of payment. The national union accepted this type of specific policy making from the local level. But it did not work through the general implications for policy making of local initiatives and a stepwise learning process.

7.4. The lack of union protection in the third experiment

The initial conditions for the third field experiment determined the union role throughout this case:

1. The project was started, with the backing of the top management of the company, and with only symbolic backing from the regional and national levels of the union.
2. The shop stewards of the experimental department were formally part of the union structure of the main company but did not have much backing from that quarter.
3. The chief shop steward of the experimental department took a very strong lead in carrying his members along with the experiment and through the first critical phase. In this way he extended the basis for local autonomy versus management, but at the same time he took considerable risks in moving ahead of regional and central union officials.

A critical incident in the third field experiment illustrates the consequences of this unbalanced support. The experimental groups had achieved encouraging results in terms of improvements measured by the six basic job design criteria and also in terms of productivity and earnings. Then some problems came up regarding the compensation for transport services. The problem was handled by the production manager of the main company who insisted on control data being gathered by work study experts. The departmental chief shop steward made it clear that this would be a waste of time and money and a strong indication that management had not understood the basic ideas of the ID project. He was able to protect the experiment from this kind of interference, with some backing from the researchers. His senior trade union colleagues were not, however, confronted strongly enough to revise their Tayloristic methods of work study and piece rates. These methods continued to be the the philosophy of production management in the main company.

A second incident two years later put the whole ID project to a critical test. The third field experiment had become something of a national model and a number of study groups had visited the field site when it became clear that growing market demands could be met only if a new and larger plant was built. Workers in the experimental groups would have to move to a new site some 10 miles away. Top management had a good chance to demonstrate their philosophy regarding participation.

The planning of the new plant went on for several months but the shop stewards and the members of the autonomous work groups were not involved in any serious way. A new manager was hired from outside without consultations. Rumours from the planning committee indicated that the conditions for autonomy in the new plant would be limited and it seemed as if top management had learnt little from the field experiment. The shop stewards brought their anxieties to the attention of the higher levels of their union but with no result. At regional level they even found that key TU representatives were against the experimental groups. They consulted the research group which in turn contacted top management and union representatives on national level.

After this intervention, local shop stewards were brought more into the planning of the new plant. Gradually, other workers from the experimental groups were involved and most of them volunteered to join the new work force, where they took key positions in the new organisation. The last phase of preparation and the starting up of the new plant with approximately 300 employees went very smoothly. Semi-autonomous work groups, with no foremen, formed the basic unit of the new organisation. There were many new problems to be solved and many of them were tackled according to principles developed by the experimental groups. However, the gap between these core groups and the management of the new plant widened over time. In spite of appeals from the shop stewards, the national union gave little support during local confrontations and finally the chief shop steward and some of the leaders from the experimental group withdrew in protest. A new shop steward committee took over representing the labour force that had had no experience of the experimental phase. Still, the basic structure of the new form of organisation was maintained. Later the trade union leaders from the experiment returned to office and took a rather strong position against what it considered a violation by management of the new principles of work organisation.

The critical incidents from the third field experiment illustrate how confrontations between management and union representatives and between TU groups on company and regional level can contribute to the policy making process. However, as long as the national unions are not prepared to react efficiently to these policy alternatives coming up in the organisational structure stagnation will occur. The risk exists that the local units will become apathetic both to policy problems emerging on local levels and to policy issues coming down the line for discussion and revision. On the other hand, it seems as if the shop steward system in Norway is a significant independent force, if committed to such ideas as those of the ID project and if they have some backing from a neutral body.

7.5. New issues for bargaining and a changing trade unions role structure in the fourth field experiment

The fourth field experiment started up under the following conditions:

1. The chief shop steward had been re-elected on a program of taking a new stand on systems of payment. In several ways his program fitted the TU policy on industrial democracy. The local TU would have to take initiatives in many concrete ways if the rank and file were to be really involved in this policy.
2. The newly appointed president of the company also had a different philosophy to his predecessors. He was deeply concerned with the organisation of work and the utilisation of human resources. He invited the shop stewards to discuss a joint plan of action to meet an economic recession which seemed likely to hit the industry soon. He stressed the need for a new management climate and new ways of educating and motivating employees for competent and responsible work.
3. Top management as well as the shop stewards' committee, on behalf of the industrial workers, agreed to the researchers' suggestion that systems of payment and supervision should not be decided upon for the new experimental plant under construction before analysis had been made of optimal task structure.

A critical incident took place when the new work organisation started to emerge on the basis of testing out the plant operations by ad hoc groups under their foremen. How were people to be paid? Could they be paid for professional skill demonstrated in shop floor operations? How could payment and training reinforce a self-perpetuating process of learning and change within the work organisation? In less than one week the action committee agreed on the basic criteria according to which the payment system should be designed. After that the payment system could easily be agreed upon. Suddenly the members of the committee realised that they had gone much further than solving a concrete problem. They had formulated important policy alternatives to be tested on the shop floor without involving either the bargaining specialists at the plant and corporate level of management or the trade union representatives at plant and national levels. The chief shop steward and the plant manager took the case to the proper bodies on higher levels and got preliminary acceptance for the new principles to be tested. However, this incident caused anxiety among the experts at higher levels of the management and union organisation. Would such initiatives on the shop floor level take away some of their power? Two years later the basic principle of workers' right to continuous learning on the job was included in the union contract bargained on national level. The basis of this contract was the payment system first worked out by the action committee.

One consequence of this event was that the local union had a number of discussions with the research team regarding the status and training of shop stewards specially to deal with local participation experiments like the one conducted in the fertilizer plant. (Special shop stewards had previously been trained for work study and safety.)

The result of these discussions was that the union concluded that it would be unwise to have a special shop steward for this purpose. Too many TU policy issues were involved and it would strengthen the local shop steward system if participation experiments became part of their general duties. Criteria were formulated against which the selection could be made of shop stewards as members of action committees:

1. full trust of employees within experimental area on the basis of their record as representatives of basic TU ideas
2. intimate knowledge of the tasks to be reorganised
3. good understanding of new principles of work organisation and ability to take part in development work from which new knowledge could be gained
4. ability to transfer experimental experience into alternative trade union policies.

Another critical incident took place when the new principles of work organisation were to be tested in a different plant in the same company. Here it became evident that new principles of supervision could not be achieved through supervisory training unless the status of supervisors and technicians were changed rather drastically. Consequently some white collar unions outside the TUC were involved. The chemical workers' union organising all the operators and skilled tradesmen had to make compromises with the other unions. Management was already aware of the increasing problems emerging from the bargaining with unions organising employees with different levels of education and different political affiliations. (While management in Norway bargains only with one industrial union organising all the blue collar workers in one company it has to bargain with several white collar and professional unions.)

The incident regarding supervisors' status in new types of work organisations became one of the major obstacles to the ID project in this particular industrial corporation. In retrospect it is clear that even if the management of the company had been more efficient in changing its policy it would have to be matched, in the not too distant future, by corresponding policy changes in the TUC and in the national unions. Such changes have not taken place, although the Trade Unions in Norway have gradually taken a new position against bureaucratic-scientific management types of organisation which were exposed as sharply in conflict with the ideals and concrete alternatives brought forward by the ID project.

When the TUC, through its special educational branch, set up the first seminars to spread the results from the four first field experiments we could clearly see that it would take time for the trade unions to digest the new ideas from the project. The form of education used to train shop stewards in bargaining, safety, time and motion studies etc. were not suitable to convey the ideas and the methods of work place democracy. When more open and flexible forms of education were tried out it sometimes turned out to initiate strong opposition to centrally controlled TU policies and practices.

There are, however, several indications that the Norwegian trade unions are not yet ready for a radical rethinking of their role and structures.

Firstly, the 1973 TUC congress discussed four different alternatives for a new TU structure in Norway. The least radical alternative would lead to a fusion of several small national unions. This would simplify the question of who is to organise which employees. The most radical alternative would lead to all union members, blue collar and white collar, on company level to join *one* union. At the moment the white collar unions and associations are separately represented at company level.

A second indication that a new TU structure will not easily emerge is the adjustment of the representative system at company level. The new law on codetermination was passed by Parliament with TUC backing, in 1972, despite our report of 1964 and without further empirical studies. To elect the representatives for the new supervisory boards and to make these bodies effective, the different unions will have to join forces on company level. Management seems to be careful not to put one union against the other in this situation. The TUC affiliated unions would seem naturally to have the strongest position in the new representative system, since they organise most of the employees. On the other hand, the first round of elections of worker representatives in 1973 showed that a very large proportion of the white collar workers exercised their voting rights, while there was only minority voting by blue collar workers in many companies. The blue collar vote was significantly lower company that had started to democratise at the shop floor level.

The third most important indication that the TU structure is not very ready for change in Norway is its new policy on work environment (work milieu). During 1973 and 1974 the TUC and the major national unions have formulated policies on work environment including health and safety, shift work and working hours, work tempo and monotony etc. That is, they have turned away from the central concern of the industrial democracy program, the democratisation of the work place (questions of alienation and authority) to what Fred Herzberg has aptly called 'the hygiene factors'.

8. Managements' role in democratisation of work

In Chapter 1 we outlined some reasons why the traditional form of organisation seemed to be ripe for revision in today's world. We will now try to be specific in our criticisms of the structural forms of this organisation.

We will limit ourselves to points which seemed to be particularly significant in the Norwegian participation experiments.

8.1. The company as a social system

The concept of the work organisation as a social system increases our understanding of interpersonal relations within the company organisation. This frame of reference has been used in many earlier studies, the Glacier studies being perhaps the best known of these (Jaques, 1950). The Norwegian field experiments provided numerous examples of how companies function as systems of interrelated functions. Some of these are worth mentioning.

In the wire-drawing experiment recruiting difficulties and high personnel turnover were related to the limited opportunities for learning and to the low degree of satisfaction offered by the jobs. In the pulp and paper plant differences in status between operators, helpers and supervisors hindered the learning and personal development we were trying to create. Status differences again acted as limiting factors when the learning of the operators had reached a higher level and impinged on the authority of supervisory and higher levels of management. In the Nobø experiment, individual participation in decision making was hampered by the limited picture each operator possessed of the overall co-ordination of tasks. The cultural expectations of women in industry also limited for some time their involvement. In the new fertilizer plant, methods of recruiting and training operators were linked with the salary and bonus system in such a way that they aided individual participation and cohesiveness of the work teams.

In all four field studies, we saw how each measure taken had eventually to be integrated with overall personnel and organisational policy. We also saw that mutual trust and willingness to try new organisational forms was more basic than any particular policy statement.

These complicated and often subtle interdependencies make it difficult or impossible to put through new job design programs on the shop floor without at the same time making changes in the wage structure, training system, and supervision. Similarly, maintaining an old system of work will inhibit change in other parts of the organisational pattern. For example, a top management which is preoccupied with co-ordination and control *within* the company will usually not allow the elbow room for learning and growth needed by operators to improve their self-management. Such management will also usually neglect the adaptation between the company and its environment whilst concentrating on elaborating internal control systems (eg. UMS for the maintenance staff).

The fact that we find connections between various sub-problems in a company is of no particular value if we cannot at the same time discover some logical order in such relationships. And we must be able to see connections between phenomena in concrete, operational terms. Looking at the company as a whole, we find it useful to categorise phenomena on different levels within the company. From this point of view, we sometimes find that the problems that exist on one level actually must be attacked from another level.

In determining what functions are on a high level and what are on a low level, one useful measure is the time span of responsibility. We normally think of functions with a time span of a month as being on a higher level than those with a one week time span. But in making this differentiation, we must see the company in its total social context, since the time span if often determined by conditions outside the company.

An example of the subtle relationship beteen phenomena is that existing between planning and supervision. If we examine problems of production planning and supervision in a plant, it is not particularly interesting merely to assert that planning is related to supervision. It can be more interesting to note that the monthly schedules from the production planning department are delivered to the shop floor in such a rigid form that a supervisor, having influence only on a weekly production cycle, cannot make the necessary adjustments to accord with that monthly planning cycle. If this is the case, the problem can be attacked successfully on the planning level, but not on the supervisory level.

Phenomena on a lower level more often call for solutions at a higher level than the other way around. Problems on the same level are usually more closely related than problems on widely separated levels. In any casc, it is not much help to state that problems are related unless we can in some way operationalise the connection. The socio-technical approach puts great emphasis on the analysis of the concrete interdependencies between parts of the total organisational system before any changes are attempted in sub systems.

8.2. The company as a socio-technical system

The concept of the socio-technical system facilitates our understanding of how we can co-ordinate two systems in the company which are regulated by different laws and processes – the technological on the one hand and the social on the other.

The technological system is ruled by the laws of the natural sciences, while the social system is ruled by principles of motivation, of learning, and so on In the former, interdependencies among elements are fixed and fully explicable with reference to universally valid laws; the interdependencies between, say, the viscosity and the temperature of oil explain how it flows through channels. This is one type of law, but there are quite different types of principles which can explain how, for example, information flows through an information network made up of human beings or how an exchange of goods and services is seen to be 'fair exchange'.

This distinction between technological and social systems may seem an elementary one, but in fact a major weakness in the traditional organisational model has been its application of purely mechanical principles in explaining the interplay between human beings and machines and even among human beings alone. Such models have been used regardless of the type of work involved and regardless of the relations between the work and those carrying out the work. We have touched on some of the unfortunate consequences of this type of thinking in Chapter 1.

The 'human relations' movement went to the opposite extreme and adopted as its quite different–though also inadequate–point of reference the relations between human beings. The Tavistock investigations during the 1950s have shown that it is absolutely necessary to take into consideration the organisation's technological aspects along with the human aspects if the organisation is to be economically viable and at the same time give its members adequate opportunities for involvement, personal growth and development.

The organisational thinking we have been using thus differs from both the purely technocratic ('scientific management') approach and the purely 'human relations' orientation.

The field experiments offered numerous instances of the interaction of the two systems and how this interaction could produce impacts in both directions, so that the effects ricocheted back and forth, producing unplanned changes both in the production process and in workers' relations with each other.

In the wire drawing department, we saw how the length of the drawing benches limited the degree of contact and co-operation among people in the department, and thus had a decisive effect on the organisational form. And we could see how the traditional narrow work roles and the lack of co-operation and cohesiveness made it difficult to cope with the problems caused by unexpected temporary variations arising in the technical production process. The partly autonomous work groups seemed better able to provide a 'joint optimisation' – that is, providing the best possible answer to both technical and human demands. (Hill, 1971, p. 72-).

In the second experiment, the measurement and handling of data on variations in paper pulp batches were of decisive influence in shaping the organisation. At the same time, we could observe how the traditional work roles made it difficult to use new communication channels and new forms of co-operation which were otherwise desirable for technical reasons.

In the third experiment, we saw the value of building up partly autonomous groups with the ability to adapt smoothly to a technical system which was comparatively simple, but which was nevertheless rather inflexible. The fourth experiment showed how the starting up of a highly mechanised fertilizer factory could be facilitated if constant efforts were made to co-ordinate technological and human considerations. New methods of differentiating and integrating work roles of communicating, training, and wage arrangements had to be created in parallel with technical requirements, in order to get a higher degree of joint optimisation of the technical and social systems.

8.3. The company as an open socio-technical system

Looking at a company as an open system can help us understand relations between the company and its environment. This was a main point of departure for our participation experiments. Since we started the experiments, it has also been explored by others, especially in organisational research of the sociological and operations – research variety.

What we mean by an open system, in contrast to a closed system, was illustrated in all the field experiments. Our looking at the companies in this way helped greatly also in understanding conditions inside the companies.

In the first experiment, we could see how the unstable labour market conditions in the company's region had a heavy impact on recruitment and wage policies. We could also see how relationships to the national employee and employer organisations affected the degree of mutual trust existing between different groups within the company. The company level groups were able to work together to some degree because of the backing each side had from the national level.

In the second experiment, it was obvious that local social conditions in that particular area were inextricably interwoven with the company's internal environment. This could be observed in the established weekly shift systems which allowed employees to spend longer consecutive periods of time on their family farms. Such an arrangement is perhaps not ideal, if we think of the manufacturing company in customary closed system terms. Seen in terms of the total environment, it was a practical way of ensuring a stable supply of labour and good relations with local suppliers of timber in a relatively isolated community where the work groups inside and social groups outside the company were strongly interdependent. Many of the employees were active members of religious movements in the area and many were actively interested in political activities. As in many Norwegian local communities the company director would not be surprised if he had to discuss tax problems with one of his workers who might well be chairman of the municipal council, on behalf of the Social Democrats. The supervisor of a department might sing in the local choir together with subordinate operators. Special group interests outside were often pretty well confined to special shift groups in the plant. One weekend we observed many of the workers at a country dance. Next week end they were on duty while a large religious meeting took place on the same spot where the dance had been. Most important also was the interdependence between the company and the local forestry interests.

The third and fourth experiments displayed sharp contrasts with regard to the type of dependency between the company and its environment. In the case of the NOBØ subsidiary we saw how the small factory was very much affected by the type of labour coming from the surrounding society. Norsk Hydro, however, was quite the opposite; all its units are of such a size and significance that they are quite dominant in their localities, in the labour market and in other ways. These two experiments present interesting contrasts of another kind; in the first, technology was on a rather low level of sophistication, and could be relatively easily rearranged, while in the second it was more complicated and mechanised, and offered few opportunities for far-reaching technical changes. In the case of Norsk Hydro, the company's transactions with the outside world were very much influenced by its special type of technology, in particular with the highly capital intensive nature of the production process. In earlier years, the technology was directly related to the region's sources of hydro power and labour was attracted to the site, while at NOBØ the small plant was sited so as to tap the local labour.

The main reason we have given so much emphasis to the interdependence between a company's internal conditions and external environments is that changes in these interdependence relations – which we can call the company's 'boundary conditions' – present severe challenges to company managements. We have often clearly seen the significance of these challenges in our field experiments. *The creation of better conditions for personal involvement in company affairs is heavily dependent on the ability of management to gain a relatively high degree of control over these boundary conditions. Otherwise, it is impossible to define the conditions within which individual persons or groups can exercise self-management.* The factors which are critical for a company's interdependence with its environment must be taken into consideration if we are to define what we have called different levels within an organisation and if we are to be able to categorise various problems and their interrelationships. Whether we rank a problem as higher level or lower level will depend on its importance in the adaptability of the organisation. This is true not only of the company as a whole, but also with regard to individual departments, where the local management will be given a corresponding responsibility to regulate boundary conditions between one department and another.

In the very first experiment, we were concerned with the fact that many of the variations in production conditions facing the wire drawing operator were essentially beyond his control. They arose from variations in departments placed earlier in the production process, in the steel works, the rolling mill, or the surface treating plant. Either management on the departmental level had to bring these variations under control or they had to be properly measured and recorded so that the experimental department could be autonomous with respect to controlling its errors. Defining the boundaries around an experimental department must be done with great care. In our pattern of organisational thinking, *management's primary responsibility lies in regulating boundary conditions – not in exercising internal control.*

In the second field experiment, we could see how the very special problems of the Norwegian timber market on the one hand, and large cyclical variations in the company's products markets, made it difficult for top and middle management, to provide stable conditions for the experimental pulp department.

In the third field experiment, the boundary conditions of the NOBØ subsidiary were quite obvious and apparently stable, until the Swedish market suddenly changed. At that point, the departmental supervision faced a difficult task in redefining the boundary conditions within which the experimental autonomous groups could function.

In the fourth field experiment, the new fertilizer plant, the boundaries were carefully examined in advance, and the department was isolated from certain potential disturbances in the surroundings which might have made it difficult to establish local self-management. Gradually, as the group system was put into operation, the protection was slowly abolished, because self-regulation on the local level had given greater adaptiveness to the company. In the longer run, it is impossible for a work group to remain isolated from other departments or from the company's environment.

Against the background of these comments, we might emphasise that local autonomy or local self-management – on the individual or the group level – does not mean that the environment is presumed to remain unchanged. Boundary conditions for a company or a department are in actuality never stable in the sense that they are unchangeable. This means that someone must see to it that transactions with the outside world are regulated in such a way that the company or the production unit can fulfill its function in its total environment and thus survive. If difficulties arise in this continuing process of adaptation the ability of management to do this is very critically dependent on the degree of self-regulation within and between the various departments. The field experiments, have been evaluated partly on the units' capacity to generate local, internal problem solving and self-regulation. In many ways, this self-regulation seems to have been improved.

If a company exists in a relatively stable environment, or if a company is the completely dominating unit in its environment, the boundary regulation will not be, in the same way, the primary task for management. Under such circumstances, the company may be more or less sufficient unto itself.

Supervision of internal conditions can be regulated in accordance with rules laid down in advance. The task of management, as we know from the study of stable bureaucratic organisations, public institutions and large, monopoly type enterprises, can quite practicably be handled in this way. In such organisations, management, in the sense we have been using the word, is scarcely needed; they are simply administered. This 'idyllic' situation now largely belongs to a past dreamtime. Not so many of the new generation of educated workers are happy to be 'simply administered'.

The degree of stability in the boundary conditions that is needed for a productive unit is one of the basic questions worth further study in order more effectively to create conditions for greater personal involvement in company operations. Our tentative conclusion is that the establishment of semi-autonomous groups is strongly dependent on the ability of management to shift its primary attention from internal co-ordination and control to the regulation of the company's boundaries. In a way, this point is in conflict with the traditional view of the task of management. In a recent study of Swedish managements, it was found that top executives habitually spent the greater part of their time on the telephone or in meetings, dealing with the company's relations with the outside world, and almost no time with their colleagues inside the company. This was interpreted as a strange, and probably defective, way of working. Our studies show, on the contrary that when boundaries are constantly changing, these changes are of vital importance to the company, and that nobody is in a better position to deal with them than top management. If, as seems quite practicable from our experiments, internal conditions can be left in the hands of relatively autonomous groups capable of looking after their own affairs, so much the better – both for the top managers (who are thus freed to maintain existing relationships and to negotiate new relationships outside the company) and for the middle management.

In the first phase of the experiments, it seemed necessary for the autonomous units to retain a certain degree of protection until they had learnt new ways of operating and of relating to the rest of the company. In the field experiments where we have succeeded best with autonomous groups, management in the initial phases put considerable emphasis on the boundary conditions, on defining group objectives, standards, resources, etc., before the experiments began. Once the experimental units acquired some stability and the groups attained positive results, the managements actually acquired increased freedom to devote themselves to looking after long term strategic boundary conditions, and thus to improve company relationships with the outside world – markets, raw materials suppliers, labour markets, and society as a whole. The companies' total adaptive ability seemed to have been improved, and might be expected to further evolve toward joint optimisation of the technological and social systems.

8.4. Management on different levels of the company

A central question in the development of an organisation will always be the optimum distribution of responsibility and authority. In Phase B of the participation experiments, we have concentrated on those aspects of authority which affect conditions in the concrete work situation. The delegation of authority and influence also raises other basic issues which are perhaps more often encountered on the supervisory and middle management levels. For example, a supervisor's responsibilities and formal status are immediately affected when influence over local working conditions is shifted to any great extent, either to partly autonomous work groups or to people in enlarged jobs. In such cases, it is more or less automatically assumed that supervisors can adapt to the new situation, that they can easily shift their attention from internal control to their relations with other departments. These are not the facts of life as we have seen them in the first experiments. Supervisors find it quite difficult to shift to a new level of control. This is partly caused by the standard pattern of middle management, partly by the history of supervision in industry.

Coming now to the middle management of companies. What is it that characterises these managers? Concepts such as supervision, middle management, and top management are constantly being used without clear distinctions being made between different types of management. We also will not attempt to give precise definitions, but only try to identify the characteristics of management which have particular significance when self-managing entities are to be established in a company. In Phase B of the project, our main emphasis has been on the conditions for concrete personal participation on the shop floor. On this level, the lack of autonomy was most obvious and unless autonomy could be improved on this level it would hinder managers from sharing decision making within the total organisation. Our first concern was hence with the supervisory level.

The concept of supervision covers the functions which, in everyday language, are carried out by the foreman. This supervision extends over both men and machines, materials and control systems. In earlier years, the supervisor was the completely dominant figure on the shop floor. He possessed competence and an overall view of operations, and – not least important – he had influence over the factors of production and the people he managed. His influence has been gradually restricted by the appearance of other forms of management control. Staff departments and specialists draw up plans and specify methods which he cannot easily change on his own initiative. Experienced and well-trained operators often know more about production technology than he does. The personnel department and shop stewards strongly restrict his handling of personnel and wage arrangements or other means he might use to motivate his subordinates. In many cases it is not at all clear to all subordinates that it is the supervisor who is responsible for the department. The very word 'subordinate' has quite another meaning in the modern industrial plant from that implied in the traditional supervisory role. Increasing self-confidence and competence and a wearing away of social class differences outside the company are influencing to a great degree conditions within the company. Less and less is it a question of people 'subordinating themselves' to others who gain their authority automatically from the positions they hold. More and more, authority is becoming a question of influence through competence, through information and through an ability to motivate people to pull together. The idea of 'pulling together' means, to be sure, that one must work within the limits of the work situation, but it also means that those who are doing the pulling are also taking part in shaping the total work situation. All this puts the supervisor in a new and difficult situation; especially in process industries and other sectors dependent on advanced technology.

If it is felt to be desirable to make the most of the increasing education and competence of the workers by developing semi-autonomous, self-managing groups the need for external supervision will further decrease. What will become of the supervisor? Internal co-ordination and control will certainly not disappear, but they will be differentiated and shared by various persons. However, it is a mistake to believe that partly autonomous groups in themselves constitute a threat to supervisors. The true situation is that there is occurring a complete re-orientation of the supervisor's position; self-management on the lower level increases the supervisor's opportunities to attend to the central task of any other manager, that is, to take care of the co-ordination between his units and the surrounding units. With this qualitative change there will also of course be radical reduction in the sheer amount of external supervision that is required. There are a number of different factors which, quite apart from the question of autonomous work groups or other more or less 'radical' organisational changes, are today working to bring about a new situation for the majority of supervisors:

1. *The organisational model* in the company is becoming more flexible and newer solutions are being placed alongside the traditional pyramidal authority structure. Both technical and social factors are producing these new alternatives.

2. *Values and norms* are slowly changing in society as a whole and will also have consequences within companies, not least in management style. The family, church, and school of yesterday, with indoctrination of traditional ideas of diligence, obedience and frugality, seem to be declining in influence. Organisations of today put more stress on justice and the individual's demands for freedom and personal development.

3. *The status system* is loosening up through a general levelling out of differences between blue collar and white collar workers and through the development of more fluid borders between unskilled workers, skilled workers, technicians, and various specialists.

4. *The structure of tasks* for supervisors is changing rapidly through the introduction of new technologies and new organisational ideas. The distribution of work, supervising, trouble-shooting and handling paper work seems to be giving way to planning and the dissemination of information, training and other personnel-administration matters.

5. *Reward and sanction systems* are changing in that authorities other than the supervisor are making decisions regarding measures to stimulate and regulate the behaviour of people. These measures themselves are gradually gaining new significance. Wages and advancement opportunities are no longer the critical elements, in the opinion of many employees. Opportunities to learn, to devote oneself to interesting, challenging work and to participate in decision making seem to be gaining rapidly in importance.

6. *The bases of recruiting and training* are being changed, most importantly for younger workers but gradually also for supervisors themselves. This applies both to the general education and technical levels that are being expected.

7. *New patterns in professional organisation* are also significant for the supervisor and his relations to both subordinates and superiors. The evolution appears to be from associations based on relatively rigid occupational demarcations and a strong central leadership towards a system with strong local shop stewards on the company level and integration of various associations and unions on the national level.

If these trends continue to evolve, what will that eventually mean for supervisors? We cannot give any definite anser to that question on the basis of our field experiments. However, some of the reactions of the foremen in these experiments may be of interest. In one of the experiments (Hunsfos), the foremen saw themselves for some time as the victims of the changes, and acted to obstruct growth and training – which as a matter of fact could have worked to improve their own situation. It has taken a great deal of time for the company to achieve an organisational pattern and a personnel policy which the foremen can accept. In the Norsk Hydro experiment the foremen also felt insecure about what the participation experiments might mean for them. No one was able to guarantee their future positions before the new organisational forms had been put to the test. Gradually, supervisors were able to become involved in investigating and obtaining some clarity about their future roles. Conferring together they saw various alternatives in future roles of supervisors:

1. 'One possibility is that the supervisor will concern himself primarily with co-ordination between his own department and adjacent departments. In other words, he would become a source of information and a planner. From time to time, he could act as the department's joint leader in the handling of important and unforeseen issues which arise suddenly and which other individuals or groups are not prepared to deal with.'
2. 'Another possibility is that the supervisor will primarily take charge of training and personnel administration questions on the departmental level.'
3. 'A third possibility is that the supervisor will become mainly a technical assistant, perhaps with special responsibility for local maintenance or local quality control.'
4. 'A fourth possibility is for the supervisor to continue to combine most of the tasks mentioned above, but this means that he will be continuing in a traditional organisational pattern. In view of the other changes which will inevitably be taking place in modern industry, his position in this case would be increasingly weak and unclear.'
5. 'A fifth alternative is for the supervisor to become absorbed into the operator group and participate in both manufacturing and supervision.'

If this was as a 'leading hand' it could hinder a general raising of the levels of self-control, co-ordination, and decision making abilities of the entire group. Some experience we have had indicates a tendency for members to leave the difficult and dangerous things to the leading hand, 'because that is what he is paid for'. It is of great importance that more experimentation and study be carried out than we could manage regarding the future role of the supervisor. The supervisors themselves as well as research and educational organisations should be involved in a collaborative effort. Basic education for supervisors will obviously have to change considerably. *From being the 'man-in-the-middle' with little hope of further advancement, the supervisory role whatever its particular form, will almost certainly emerge as the first level of management.* Moreover, company personnel policies must provide support for a planned transition into new supervisory roles that will meet the six criteria for them, but not at the expense of others.

The middle manager in production seems, in the evolving modern organisations, to be acquiring a clear cut primary task – that of striving for the optimal utilisation of the financial, material and human resources for which he is responsible. He can gradually step back from directing the supervision of machines, raw materials and employees and concentrate on managing by objectives, making good use of the control techniques and methods which are effective with respect to the available resources. The time perspective for his work will thus be expanded. The middle manager must participate in the design of operational programs for various departments and keep a running check on the utilisation and administration of resources and the attainment of goals within his area of responsibility. Together with the other middle managers he must be able to contribute to the development of policies that affect his sector and co-ordination between them. He must assist his working groups and their supervisor-co-ordinators to interpret the control principles and current policies. He must be able to constantly stimulate the growth of competence and organisational structures so as to increase the effective human resources available to the company.

In the developing organisation, it will be more and more common for production managers and others on the middle management level to join temporary project groups established to serve a purpose extending beyond their own department or function. When the special objectives of such a group have been achieved, the group can dissolve and the members return to their usual roles. Members of these project groups will be recruited from different sectors and levels of the company, with the occasional addition of outside specialists. Once the practice of wearing more than one hat becomes well accepted, it will be possible to progress gradually to what is called a 'matrix organisation'.

In the field experiments we have seen clear examples of the decisive role played by production management in the transition to a new organisational form. If they are known to believe that increased self-management, by their subordinates, is both feasible and desirable it can contribute very heavily to the successful introduction of such self-management principles. But management can also, of course, affect the course of events in the opposite direction. A lack of public commitment, of receptivity to suggestions from below or sluggishness in putting new arrangements into practice, can very quickly stifle initiative on the local level. When that happens, and the subordinates lose interest in the experiments and faith in the new ideas, managers will find confirmation of their negative feelings towards the new ideas and justification for the belief that control from above is the only workable management method. A manager who is receptive to initiatives from colleagues and subordinates will very likely have this positive position strengthened by the reaction. Although, not before he has been tested for his genuineness.

These comments on the role of production management are not intended to cover the entire subject of management's influence on our participation experiments. We do not, in fact, have sufficient data from the experiments to make a really exhaustive analysis of such questions. We have, however, wished to draw attention to a few points which make it easier to discuss the principal tasks of managers, on different levels, in those situations where there is a desire to increase the degree of self-management in the company. Without some knowledge of these principal tasks of management, it is difficult to shape an overall organisational policy and to plan the training and development measures necessary for increasing the degree of self-management. If supervision and production management do not support self-management and autonomy on the shop floor, the normal centralised decision making and control processes will continue as before, regardless of any expressed top level policy regarding expanded autonomy. At the same time, management cannot be decentralised to any great degree unless the structure of jobs and co-ordination is changed on bottom levels, that is, unless conditions for involvement and personal growth are improved.

The role and number of specialists in larger companies has become increasingly important. This development has sometimes caused concern that a company's other employees will be relegated to the most routine jobs. However that may be, it is certain that a steadily increasing number of persons will be finding work in professional, specialist categories because of improved opportunities for professional education in computers, business analysis and so forth. The actual evolution will, however, depend to a great degree of how essential it is felt to be to improve conditions for personal participation at all levels in the company – including the professional levels. If development turns out not to be in this direction, specialisations at the staff level might well proliferate and crystallise in the way the crafts did in the British industrial revolution. Gradually, the majority of specialists would be working on quite a low level and would be able to use relatively little of their professional knowledge.

If work organisations move in the direction we have been exploring then there is the possibility that future staff specialists will be characterised by a high level of utilisation of knowledge, techniques and skills, and would be only rarely involved in the details of problem solving, manufacturing systems, service or control. As before, their role could be of a consultative rather than an executive character. However, even this distinction would be eroded at the policy forming level with a move toward the 'matrix organisation'. In these forms of organisation people with various types of skills rotate between various roles in accordance with shifting demands in the work situation and with little concern for whom is staff or line. Moreover, it should be quite natural for specialists not to feel themselves exclusively identified with the company organisation. Their strong orientation toward professional associations and institutions for education, research and development will be one way for companies to make sure that the specialists keep up with developments in their fields. It will also mean a great deal in maintaining the professional people's independence.

We have already been able to see something of these changes in staff roles in personnel, work study and production planning.

Top management in the company will, in line with our comments on supervision, middle management and staff specialists, also gain some clarity of function. The company management's main job seems to be in handling, together with the board of directors, the relations between the company and its environment. If top management is often forced to intervene into matters of internal regulation or control, it will gradually slide over toward doing the job of middle management and to that extent its handling of its primary job will be neglected.

In some companies, the managing director seems to be able, by sheer personal strength and ability, to fulfill this primary function, with some assistance from the board of directors (which in Norway usually consists of the managing director plus three to five outsiders). One man leadership arrangements of this or similar types will, however, become increasingly untenable in companies of any size. Gradually, as a company's activity becomes more comprehensive and more complicated, to cope with a more rapidly changing social environment, it will in most cases be forced to adopt a team approach involving the many forms of competence available to management. Every company is influenced by certain external technical, marketing, and social conditions, and when these conditions shift, top management must adapt itself in line with the changing needs. What we seem to be getting is a change both in the behaviour of top management as well as in its relation to the board. The board must be composed in such a way – and must acquire the confidence of others, both internally and externally and externally, in such a way – that it can make available the resources, and help create the working conditions that will allow the company to survive. The board must also see to it that resources are allocated to new activities when the company's existing activities are no longer viable in the given social environment.

We suggest that, much more than in the past, boards of directors must ask of each of their decisions 'what will this do to enhance the opportunities for our employees to develop and realise their potentialities?' It is the board in the first instance, not the top management, that must ask the question 'should we stay in our current business if we cannot make more human use of our human resources?' Whilst a board must respect the area of command of its managing director it ought to provide him with an explicit and unambiguous statement of their philosophy on the management of human resources. The statement should leave no doubt in the managing director's mind about his responsibility in this matter nor the backing he can expect.

Top management must be strategically oriented in order to continually approach an optimal ultilisation of the company's total resources, technical and human. Optimization cannot be sought by reference to some eternally valid set of objectives, e.g. profit level. Nevertheless, strategic objectives can be defined with sufficient precision to give a concrete idea of the important interdependencies which must always be sustained between the company and its environment and which must be held somewhat stable if the optimalization process is to be carried out. Company 'objectives' are usually discussed in rather broad, loose terms – the necessity to make a profit, and to survive. But these overall objectives can much more meaningfully be broken down into their component parts. We now tend more and more to think of objectives in operational terms, which we can derive from the concrete interdependencies we mentioned. For example, a company must rely on others for certain raw materials deliveries, on a certain willingness to exchange technical know-how, and on the continuing demand of others for its products or services. Entities outside the company in all these areas must, of course, be able to rely on the company. There is a whole range of interdependencies between the company and its environment – in marketing, in financing, in the labour market, in the educational area, and so on – and the objectives of the company can be expressed in terms of these interdependencies. When a company radically changes its own ability to respond by increasing internal self-management at all levels this means there must be a revision of the company's objectives. But it does not mean that everyone takes responsibility for everything.

Divisions of responsibility and authority on various levels within the organisation must be defined in such a way that sections are not disturbed by things that they could in any case not do anything about, or at least not until someone else has first done something. Stability, however, does not mean a static situation. Quite contrary, it implies a constant process of adaptation between allocation and co-ordination of internal social and technical resources and the changes taking place in the environment. It is a question of controlled active adaptation which can take different forms, varying according to environmental conditions and the company's special characteristics.

The viewpoints on management which we have presented here may seem overly condensed and abstract. But we have wanted to touch on this subject, however briefly, because observers who have become interested in the concept of self-management and semi-autonomous groups almost invariably ask, 'What about management?' We can answer that the organisational thinking we used as our point of departure seemed from the beginning to point in the directions outlined above. So far, nothing in the field experiments has led us to change our basic hypotheses; neither have they progressed to the point where we can rest on a set of generally valid conclusions. However, there is scarcely any doubt that the whole complex of management problems will have to be viewed in a new light if the new organisational principles we have been discussing become widely accepted. A concept such as 'semi-autonomous groups' is in itself incompatible with the traditional idea of authoritarian management; management that delegates no more authority than it absolutely has to, and then puts the delegated authority on a mere shoestring of time span of responsibility.

The field experiments with partly autonomous groups seem to put the questions of the proper degree of stratification and distribution of responsibility in an entirely new perspective. Traditional organisational forms, with extensive use of job descriptions and instructions seem to involve a heavy emphasis on who is personally responsible to whom and where individual responsibility shall lie when something goes wrong. These traditional thinking patterns also suggest that each person must report to only one superior and that each superior can control only a number of subordinates sufficiently small to enable adequate personal control. We wind up with a steeply pyramidal and heavily stratified organisational structure, with numerous dividing lines between areas of authority. In capital-intensive process industries the potential costs of failing to personally supervise others has had a markedly steepening effect on the pyramid.

The socio-technical approach implies a radically different view of the organisation. Indeed, it emphasises, not the sharp differentiations between jobs, but the interdependencies among tasks. With this as a point of departure, we can take care that the organisation is designed so that authority to control an activity is placed where control can most effectively be carried out – at whatever level in the organisation. This central idea of the socio-technical system can be a determining factor in shaping the structure of the organisation and the levels it may contain. The organisation thus becomes *task*-oriented rather than *person*-oriented. The psychological job demands we have discussed, as well as the requirements of the technology itself, seem to indicate that the influence which has traditionally been placed higher up in the organisation should be moved much further down and quite often right down to the shop floor. In principle, this is what has been called 'delegation of responsibility'. What is new in the field experiments is that they seem to give more systematic knowledge of the *technological and social conditions necessary for such delegation of authority*. A decisive element is the fact that the reallocation of responsibility provides, on the whole, better control of the system – its boundary conditions as well as its internal variations – without requiring the human beings involved to be controlled by coercion.

Regarding the steepness or flatness of the organisational 'pyramid', this will depend on the time perspective contained in the decision making process. A certain stratification seems necessary in order to give the management group the tranquility necessary for them to concentrate on studying and adjusting the long term trends. But internal communication seems best served by an organisation so 'flat' that the whole idea of an organisational pyramid can perhaps lose its overall significance. The levels of management (as distinct from levels of remuneration) between top management and the new supervisor-co-ordinator should be no more than the number of Chinese boxes that net the latter's decision making into the former's.

Regardless of how the question of stratification in the organisational pattern is resolved, the field experiments have shown that responsibility and authority must follow one another. No one will willingly take responsibility for something he has no authority over. No one will readily trust another with authority for which he is not responsible. This applies both on the individual level and the group level.

The objection may be raised that semi-autonomous groups will not behave responsibly toward the overall organisation and its primary objectives. That is, the group may be inclined to look only after its own interests. In answer to this, we may note, first, that if this were true it would by no means be a defect unique to partly autonomous groups; the formation of cliques in opposition to the organisation's goals is already a well known phenomenon in traditional organisations which include detailed control over subordinates by supervisors and upper level managers. Second, what we have referred to as 'boundary control' means that the groups are constantly being kept aware of those variations in the surrounding environment to which they must adjust their actions. They seem, because of this, to become not only more willing but more able to adapt themselves to the constantly shifting demands of the situation. Ability and willingness to bend to the demands of purely formal authority become less needed. Our experience shows that members of semi-autonomous groups are more inclined to adapt their efforts to the overall goals of the company than they were when they worked in relatively narrow jobs under strict supervisory control. Failure of groups to responsibly exercise their authority could only result in reversion to traditional supervisory controls.

It is probably true that loyalty and unity in a company is traditionally associated with the personal qualities of the management. We think that the shift in work ethos undermines this and makes it more necessary for management to formulate the objectives for the company in such a way that they concretely express values and norms with which employees can easily identify. If we look back at the job requirements, we can see that this is one of the points they cover. It is completely decisive for loyalty and unity that the company and its activities bear the stamp of an institution which handles relations with the environment in a way that is accepted and respected both internally and externally. Selznick (1957) has described how an institutionally stamped management is dependent on a commonly accepted view of overall goals and on norms of behaviour that are accepted and encouraged. Unity within the management group regarding the company's objectives and norms of behaviour have a decisive impact on the feelings of loyalty and unity that exist in the company as a whole. The field experiments indicate that groups on the shop floor as well as higher up in the organisation system find it difficult to liberate themselves from earlier ways of thinking and habitual defensive positions, and are thus less capable of working together to solve problems on the local level. This difficulty is particularly enhanced if they do not feel that top management as well as middle management and supervisors understand and fully accept the objectives and the principles that lie behind the experiments. Obviously, the unions and shop stewards must also be seen to support the experiments and the fundamental thinking that lies behind them.

Gradually, as we accumulate concrete examples, it will make it easier for those contemplating similar projects to see to what extent personnel and organisational policies have to be clarified beforehand. In the fourth field experiment, a new personnel policy framework and a change of course in the entire company's policy was being announced by management at the same time the experiment was starting. Gradually, as the experiments develop, new company policies will be tested and further refined through concrete decisions. Naturally, this does not mean that all levels of the organisation can be quickly and easily brought into line with such new principles as those involved in our experiments. Particularly in a large company, it can take a considerable time for new objectives and new behaviour norms to become worked into company operations. Whether the process is successful depends partly on the capacity of the new organisational forms themselves to justify their existence under practical operational conditions. But it also depends on the willingness and ability of management to nurture and adjust where necessary, the new forms in the company and to stimulate their growth through important well-timed strategic decisions and in day-to-day operations.

The picture we have given here to some principal questions that face management in systematically introducing participation does not, of course, cover all the issues that may arise. The same reservation applies to the points of organisational theory we have touched upon. Our main intention has been to show that not all types of organisational thinking – and not all management philosophies – are compatible with participation projects which aim at improving conditions for personal involvement. We have mentioned some rather new organisational concepts only because participation experiments require that those who take part must have a certain *conceptual support* for the programs they are carrying out. One must have a coherent conceptual apparatus in order to think and act consistently and in line with a well defined policy. One must also have *attitudinal support* – a feeling that others are supporting the efforts, that they welcome the new ideas and are prepared to act despite a certain risk of failure. Finally, one needs interpersonal or *social support* in a program of change – so that, for example, the re-organisation of any single job harmonises with changes brought about at the same time in other workers' roles. Similarly, a re-organisation of duties and occupational requirements on the management level must fit in with the changes being made in the shop steward network and training programs.

9. Strategies for industrial change

9.1. The basic steps in the Norwegian Industrial Democracy Project

The first step was to de-mythologise the notion that industrial democracy was necessarily, or even usefully, identified with specific forms of worker *representation* (Emery and Thorsrud, 1964).

In the next phase the major task was that of diffusing and further developing social scientific solutions. This involved us in the following process.

1. Establishment of a Joint Committee representing labour and management was the first step, taken already in 1962 (before phase A started). This body was designed to assist the researchers in planning, initiating, carrying out and evaluating the research. The joint committee proved to be of particular importance in the initiation and evaluation phases. Also at certain critical points of change the joint committee played an active and important role. One aspect of this role was the support they gave to the managers and local union officials who had to accept the responsibility for experimental changes in their plants. Another aspect was the assurance given by the continued presence as an appeal body and a potential source of sanctions in case major issues arose that were best dealt with at a higher level than that of the organisation involved in the field experiment.

2. Choice of experimental company was undertaken in collaboration with the joint committee mentioned above and the management and union inside the company. The choice of company was made on the basis of criteria set up by the researchers and agreed by the committee. The main criteria have been the type of technology and product, the position of the company in the branch, the geographic location of the company and the level of labour-management relations inside the firm. These were thought to affect the relevance, potential influence and the possibility of successful change.

3. A systematic analysis of each selected company was made in order to get a general outline of the critical variations between the company (as a system) and its environment; its product markets, input of raw materials, contact to technological developments in research and education, the financial situation, marketing relations and finally the labour market and other links to community institutions. The companies assisted with these analyses. In this we were concerned with going beyond the question of 'willingness to change' to the question of ability to tolerate extended experimental changes in the face of environmental demands and pressures.

4. *Choice of experimental sites* within the companies was made in collaboration with management and the shop stewards of the plant. The choice was influenced by the kind of technology involved, the strategic position of the department inside the company, and the attitude of management and employees toward experimenting along these lines. As far as possible we wanted a site with a fairly clearly defined boundary but also well placed, strategically, for subsequent diffusion of the results.

This meant that improvements in the control of variation inside one department should be readily experienced as advantageous for the preceding and subsequent phases of production. This would be likely to interest them in trying to achieve similar changes in their own departments.

5. *Establishing action committees* with representatives of operators, supervisors, factory and departmental management proved to be crucial for the continuance of the field experiments. In the beginning of the experiments the research group were very active but gradually the action committees had to assume full responsibility for the carrying out of the research project inside the company. This appeared to be a pre-requisite for the involvement of the operators.

6. *Socio-technical analyses of the experimental sites* were undertaken in co-operation with the action group and company specialists. The major steps in the socio-technical analyses can be summarized as follows:

a. The analysis starts with a description of the variations in inputs and outputs of the department and measurements of the significant sources of variation in quality and quantity during transformation of the inputs. Estimates are made also of departmental capabilities. Measurements include e.g. variations in services, technical equipment, personnel and management.
b. Drawing upon the experience of operators, management and specialists

we seek to get estimates of the relative importance of different variations which have been registered during the first step. Usually a matrix can be constructed that shows the relations between the different kinds of variation. This is the most effective way of identifying task interdependence that are not reflected in the current structuring of responsibilities and power, or which require technical change. These matrices are also valuable in identifying production sub-systems and in identifying the criteria actually being used for judging the importance of critical variation. These criteria operationally define the primary task of the department and make it possible to set up an effective system for feedback of results.

c. A description of the formal organisation in terms of positions, work roles, recruitment and training.
d. Analysis of the communication network, partly through interviews, partly through observations, and partly through analysis of record flows. The aim is to construct a conceptual model of the network and to test it against various independent sources of evidence.
e. Systematic interviews with personnel to get a base-line measure of satisfactions and dissatisfactions with the old system. The attitude survey is usually structured around the basic psychological job requirements. In this way we have a chance to measure what the improvements of conditions for personal participation actually take place.
f. Analysis of wage and salary system to see how well it reflects current distributions of effort and responsibility. The fit between these has to be one of the guidelines in inducing greater personal participation.

7. The company policy usually has to be described in concrete terms with respect to such management practices as job allocation, training and job incentives and also with respect to their product markets for raw materials, 'know how', labour, capital and products. In defining company policy, we have found it necessary to identify how and by whom policy is made because experimentation in generating units usually invokes questions of company policy.

8. Program for change is drafted in co-operation with the personnel of the chosen department and the company specialists. The action group plays a major role in formulating and presenting the program for change. Typical features of a change program are:

a. Multi-skilling of operators so that they can alternate between different work roles inside partly autonomous work groups. This is usually needed because of the prevalent philosophy of one man/one skill.

b. Development of the measures of variations and of the data analysis methods needed for control by the operators. This is often necessary because control has been traditionally held at a level which is too removed to undertake quick and detailed control action and hence has not needed the requisite information. In one case the establishment of a new information room was a major part during one phase of an experiment.

c. Attachment of a local repair man to back up the quick and detailed control actions for which the operators are expected to assume responsibility.

d. Institutionalising the meetings, contacts, etc. that enable the operators, as a group, to plan and co-ordinate their activities.

e. Training the foremen to supervise, co-ordinate and plan for the activities of groups rather than individuals. This usually means an extension of their time span of responsibility and some skilling in tasks of appraisal, diagnosis and planning of production that are traditionally located at middle management level.

f. Design and introduction of new bonus arrangement if the department has or needs some special kind of incentive schemes. The analysis of variation in terms of quality and quantity will usually have been done during previous phases of analysis and can now be applied as a basis for an incentive to work and learn as a group with regard to a wide spectrum of departmental objectives.

9. Institutionalisation of a continued learning and organisational change process is the final stage of the development project. Gradually the change process, and the responsibility for it must shift from the action committee to the management and shop stewards or be otherwise assigned to formal parts of the work organisation in terms of standing committees etc. This can only be accomplished by embodying the lessons of the experiment in the philosophy or style of management by making appropriate organisational changes.

10. Diffusion of results has been an objective of all the experimental studies undertaken in the Industrial Democracy project. It has been clearly understood by the experimental companies that they would carry a certain responsibility of helping the research to be known inside the branch and the industry as such. The central joint committee took a major responsibility for the diffusion process, together with the researchers, but it was obviously going to be necessary for the experimental plants to act as demonstration sites. Gradually the researchers would have to take less responsibility for the diffusion of results and concentrate mainly on reanalysis and reformulation of the hypothesis and principles that formed the basis of these experiments.

Most of the above steps were necessary in the four experiments we have run so far as part of the Industrial Democracy Project. Rather than looking at each of these steps as part of a cookbook recipe, one should look at each step as a condition for change; sometimes the sequence will change and sometimes the content of each point will take a particular form according to the particular situation in the company or experimental departments.

The abovementioned points can be summarised in four basis aspects of change, namely:

1. Information
2. Involvement
3. Commitment
4. Actual social change

9.2. Steps for change in the seventies

In the preceding section we have outlined the basic steps we found most productive for diffusion in Norway through the sixties. *If we were back in the early sixties, starting again, would we do it the same way*?

This has been a matter of many earnest discussions between ourselves and our colleagues. (Philip Herbst, 1974). The very rapid diffusion in Sweden after 1968-69 did not in general follow these steps.

Developments in Sweden went rather as follows:

1. Some common networks started to grow between Norway and Sweden in the mid sixties, among action researchers, trade unionists and managers. A common understanding of needs for democratisation of work and some new approaches developed.
2. When the first (Industrial Democracy) field experiments had come under way in Norway similar systematic developments started in Sweden sponsored by a joint Council of participation (TU/Management).
3. In 1969, the report on the first four Norwegian experiments was presented

publicly in Sweden and given considerable publicity. The Swedish Confederation of Employers and the Trade Union Council sponsored publication of the report and took an active part in public debate of Industrial Democracy; different forms and approaches.

4. Both the major parties in industry started to inform their members of the recent experiences in democratisation of work. Employers concentrated on informing and activating professional groups. Trade unions gave general information to members and some shop steward training.
5. A great number of limited projects (and some extensive ones) started in a great number of firms in the early seventies. Some started with changes in job design, job rotation etc. Others started with new salary and wage systems and perhaps educational programs – others again with new types of information and communication programs, sometimes linked to new bodies of labour-management participation. Methods of personnel management and 'rationalisation' were changed to improve participation etc. The implicit strategy was that whatever the first measures might be they could always be supplemented by new and complementary ones. The more intensive Norwegian and Swedish experiments were visted by numerous study groups.
6. A flow of information, methods and people started to spread across companies and professional groups, educational institutions and trade unions.

This process of change in Sweden is in many respects open ended and likely to produce its own particular problems.

We find that we have ourselves made many variations in how we now proceed, in several countries including Norway. Still we do not find it easy to give an answer. As a start, let us consider the sorts of changes we have felt it desirable to make in order to get better diffusion.

Table IX. 1. Comparison of change principles.

Norway 1962-9	Our current tendencies (1975)
1. (Point 1 p. 150) Sanctioning at a level higher than & inclusive of the values of the contending parties.	Still our ideal. Short of this ensuring local management-union agreement. Hopefully goin a step further to get management at least to publicly state its commitment to values that are inclusive of management and labour interests.

2/3/4. (p. 150-151) Deliberate and expert selection of demonstration sites to maximise representativeness, willingness and ability to change. In essence a small number of concentrated thrusts at key sectors with a view to minimising failures.	Choice not selection. We are no longer willing to assume that we know where change will have most diffusion value. Nor to judge ability to change. Willingness to make a start is now the only criteria. In essence a willingness to move over a broad front, accepting that the ability of many may not match their willingness and that many may turn out to have very little diffusion value. Maximising successes more relevant than minimising failures.
5/6/8. (p. 151-152) Work via action committees, with collaboration of experts to achieve a list, a program of of changes.	'Participative redesign'. (See appendix 1 for a detailed spelling out of this.)
7. (p. 152) Company policies stated for concrete issues of job allocation training etc.	A statement of the values that will guide the company's decisionmaking.
9. (p. 153) Gradually shifting responsibility for change to within the organisation.	Agreed, but this principle should not need to be invoked if design process starts with the particpative model.
10. (p. 153) Responsibility for diffusion shifting from national body to the companies as demonstration sites.	Establishing from the beginning that diffusion is located in a network of 'friendly neighbours'. The initial companies help the newcomers; not refers them to their 'doctor'.

Running through those changes is the emphasis on the greater participation of the people whose jobs are under consideration. With this goes a playing down of the role of socio-technical experts and of the significance of an integrated plan.

We can now try to give the reasons for the changes. Firstly, the ideas inspring the changes are no longer novel and practically untried as they were in the early sixties. Then the ideas and their testing had to be carefully nurtured and protected. From about 1969 we were into a qualitatively different phase of the diffusion process (Emery, 1974b). Secondly, we were working in a very different social climate. The rising of the Paris students in May 1968 signified a great decline in the general acceptability of authoritarianism in any form. Those exercising authority in industry were confronted, even in their own families, with a new spirit of self-determination. Lastly, we had gradually forged a kit of conceptual tools that could be readily grasped and used by people at all levels, particularly if applied to their own daily work experience. (See Appendix 1). Of course, an element of mutual trust between workers and management is implied if the former accept to use these concepts to redesign their work. A breakdown in the long term pattern of full employment might erode such trust as there is and jeopardise the developments we report herein. But there seems to be no way that the clock will run backwards to the old under-educated, male dominated, subservient work-force.

Appendix 1. A participative approach to the democratisation of the work place

This appendix first appeared in early 1974 as *Participative Design: work and community life*, by Fred and Merrelyn Emery, Canberra, Centre for Continuing Education, Australian National University.

We have appended it because it is the best proven one way of going further along the path we trod in Norway. The first part spells out the basic kit of conceptual tools that workers and management need to get to grips with in redesigning their own work. The second part reports on the practical problems of *organising workshops* for redesigning work.

Part I: The human dimension of work

We have a sound body of knowledge on which to design jobs and organisations so that they meet technical and economic requirements. Here we will suggest how we can design our jobs so that they *also* meet human requirements.

Bureaucratic structures and the systems of management associated with them have been unable to systematically provide for the personal growth and development of their members, in particular the large numbers at the base of the pyramid, who may even be degraded by their work experiences (e.g. assembly-line workers, shorthand typists in typing pools). The traditional conception of management's task has been inhibitive of such growth.

'The philosophy of management by direction and control . . . is inadequate to motivate because the human needs on which this approach relies are today unimportant motivators of behaviour. Direction and control are essentially useless in motivating people whose important needs are social and egotistic . . . People, deprived of opportunities to satisfy at work the needs which are now important to them, behave exactly as we might predict – with indolence, passivity, resistance to change, lack of responsibility, willingness to follow the demagogue, unreasonable demands for economic benefits'.[1]

1. McGregor, D. *The Human Side of Enterprise*, N. Y., McGraw-Hill, 1960.

Cumulative investigations in Europe, North America, Australia and Scandinavia have enabled social scientists to identify a number of important determinants of job satisfaction, located both in the dynamics of man-task relations and in the social climate of the work situation. These factors have been called 'psychological job requirements'. The first three concern job content involving the concept of optimality which is descriptive of differences between individuals and within individuals over time.

1. Adequate elbow room. The sense that they are their own bosses and that except in exceptional circumstances they do not have some boss breathing down their necks. Not so much elbow room that they just don't know what to do next.
2. Chances of learning on the job and going on learning. We accept that such learning is possible only when men are able to set goals that are reasonable challenges for them and get a feedback of results in time for them to correct their behaviour.
3. An optimal level of variety, i.e. they can vary the work so as to avoid boredom and fatigue and so as to gain the best advantages from settling into a satisfying rhythm of work.
4. Conditions where they can and do get help and respect from their work mates. Avoiding conditions where it is in no man's interest to lift a finger to help another: where men are pitted against each other so that 'one man's gain is another's loss;' where the group interest denies the individual's capabilities or inabilities (as in the bull gang system that used to characterise Australian dock work and is apparently still prevalent in New Zealand Meat Freezing Works).
5. A sense of one's own work meaningfully contributing to social welfare. That is, not something that could as well be done by a trained monkey or an industrial robot machine. Nor something that the society could probably be better served by not having it done, or at least not having it done so shoddily.
6. A desirable future. Quite simply, not a dead end job; hopefully one that will continue to allow personal growth.

We have assumed, from our past experience, that these psychological requirements *cannot* be much better met by simply fiddling with individual job specifications, e.g. job enlargement, job rotation, rest pauses, humane supervisory contacts. If the nature of the work allows room for improvement this will be best achieved by locating responsibility, for control over effort and quality of personal work and for interpersonal co-ordination, with the people who are actually doing the job.

We think that the reasons for the proven superiority of the 'group solution' have emerged, rather painfully, over the past thirty-five years of laboratory and field experiments. The differences in the structural relations of men, tasks and supervisors gives us our first and most important clues, e.g. Figures 1 and 2.

Figure 1 pretty precisely defines what has become the dominant bureaucratic form of organisation that has been enthusiastically installed by production engineers and O. and M. experts alike. It is scientific management. Control and co-ordination, the two dimensions of human organisation, are vested in the supervisor. He controls his subordinates by specifying what each individual A, B, C, etc. will do vis-a-vis the task allotted to him, X, Y, Z, etc. Co-ordination is the supervisor's preserve. Achievement of his section's task will almost certainly be related to the adequacy of co-ordination because of either interdependence between the tasks themselves (as exemplified in process industries) or variations in optional work loads between individuals (as exemplified in typing pools). The short term fluctuations in his section's performances are not easy to manage as the supervisor increasingly loses his right to hire and fire. Co-ordination is the variable he can manipulate and hence manipulate the image his supervisor has of him. This is not without its difficulties.

Figure 1

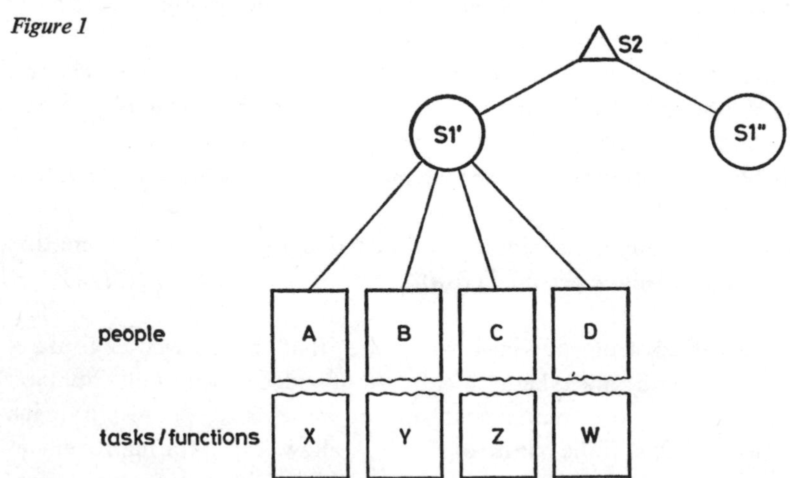

Figure 2

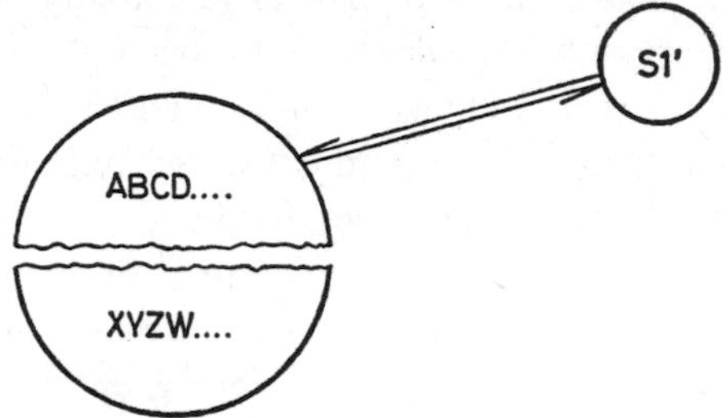

Tight job specifications to give him greater control of his subordinates can also be used by them, particularly if they are unionised, to cramp his style when he seeks to use their idle time to help out on other jobs. Amongst employees, in this system there will be an almost universal tendency to develop an 'informal system' to turn the requirements of co-ordination to their advantage, e.g.

1. 'Dargs' and other restrictive but informal production norms to reduce the productive potential with which the supervisor might do some shuffling.
2. Cliques whereby subgroups in the section ease their jobs by collaring for themselves the productive potential in co-ordination. Because the purposes of these cliques are personal they tend to organise themselves around bases for common trust i.e. religion, race, old school. They do not tend to organise themselves around the interdependencies of task and personal work capabilities that particularly effect the supervisor's concern, namely his section's productive capability. They are after the cushy jobs.

We can easily sum up this description. The building brick for this type of organisation is the one man-shift unit. Controls might be sloppy or tight but the principle is the same. The organisational module is the supervisor and his section; with responsibility for co-ordination being jealously defended as the prerogative of the supervisor. The module and its basic building brick can be indefinitely repeated upwards to the managing director and his directly reporting functional managers. It is the organisational design that has been used by the western world to go into large scale production. It happens to be the organisational form that put up the pyramids and China's Great Wall. It is based on the premise that human beings can be used as redundant parts.

This rather wordy description of figure 1 might help to show why redefinition of individual jobs has no real chance of changing things; why it is so much favoured by some managements and arouses suspicions of some unions. Enrichment of individual jobs usually entails switching bits of task X from A to B etc. This can easily generate into 'robbing Peter to pay Paul'. Very difficult if Peter happens to be in a craft union.

Such manipulation leaves the power structure and communication pattern basically unchanged. If A, confronted with new circumstances, believes that he needs some help from B or that he is picking up some information of potential value to B the communication is still up to the supervisor and, as he sees fit, down to the subordinates. The communication which is needed to reflect and cope with changing task requirements is being channelled through through a filter/amplifier system that is labelled on one side 'us', and on the other side 'them'. The goals of the supervisor are those that concern his section's overall performance and explicitly no business of his subordinates, A B C . . . The subordinates' goals concern the performance standards set for sub-tasks X, Y, Z, etc. This means that communications are going to be amplified and attenuated in the same taskrelated channel, by different criteria. The 'us's' will amplify what makes them look good vis-a-vis their own task performance or relative to their 'colleagues'. They will hear as little of the downward communication as suits them and they can get away with. The supervisor will be anxious to hear and remember what will sound good to his supervisor, including excuses for malperformance.

The power structure is similarly unchanged. Someone once said that 'What Caesar can do, Caesar can undo'. The redefining of individual job specifications for 'job enrichment' is very much within the traditional managerial prerogatives. Come the usual crisis and the demands to tighten up, and the same managerial prerogatives enable the individual jobs to be screwed back to tight, specialised, supervisable performances that will yield a guaranteeable performance level. The variation seems little different to the fluctuations between sloppy and tight rates in the individual incentive schemes we see in light engineering works. Little wonder that the engineering unions have been foremost in expressing scepticism about 'job enrichment'.

The *alternative organisational module* (Figure 2) has markedly different potentials. The first and obvious feature is that it is not restricted to just redistributing jobs X, Y, Z etc. between A, B, C etc. It allows for A, B, C etc. to share and allocate amongst themselves the requirements for control and co-ordination of their task-related activities. Thus it is not just the sum of the individual tasks X, Y, Z etc. that they take responsibility for. It is also all the task interdependencies (interactions) XY, XZ, YZ, XYZ . . . Also, and of critical importance in the kind of jobs produced by the widespread adoption of the bureaucratic model, is the fact that the group must share the tasks of monitoring and controlling the contributions of its own members, and organising their mutual support to cope with individual and task variations. In this module individual 'job enrichment' has a qualitatively different scope. It does not require that everyone has to have his job enriched to the same degree. As a desirable flow on it provides the individual with a human scale of organisation (a work 'home' and 'family' territory) whereby he feels he fits into the corporation, no matter how large that may be. It provides him with an on-the-job defensive and offensive group of colleagues such that his work life will not easily be degraded at the whim of a new, go-getting manager, or because his corporation has run into yet another of its budgetary crises. Communication and power within these groups take on markedly different characteristics to what we find in bureaucratic organisation – which is why communication and power cannot be taken as basic variables of organisational design (they are universally present attributes of organisation, but they do not tell us much of relevance about what is communicated).

Changes in organisational design affect the nature of communication and power *but the reverse does not hold.* Provided we have a group and not just a collection of individuals or a mob, and provided that the group has accepted responsibility for a group task, then it will seek to make its life easier (or more productive for their ends) by:

1. communicating quickly, directly and openly the needs for co-ordination arising from task or individual variability
2. by allocating tasks and other rewards and punishments to control what they consider to be a fair contribution by members.

Such groups can get a sense of an over-riding group responsibility only if they have at least four members (with three it is too often a matter of just interpersonal relations – two against one). If the groups are kept to eight or under they are less prone to 'group emotional' (mob) behaviour. Larger groups can be very effective if they share a deep-rooted work culture and the parts of the group task are highly interdependent (e.g. the eighteen man team in Australian Rules football).

These groups can be only semi-autonomous, not fully autonomous, as they often were in cottage industry. They are working with materials and equipment for which the company is responsible for getting an adequate return. They are working in conditions where the company is responsible, not them, for observing the mass of social legislation laid down for basic pay rates, safety, product quality, pollution etc.

Many circumstances indicate that varying degrees of autonomy will be agreed to for different working groups. At the lowest levels of autonomy the groups may simply have the right to decide on working methods and allocation of work between themselves. At a somewhat higher level they may control some of the conditions from which they start, e.g. membership of their groups, equipment and tools, maintenance, planning and estimating, quality levels for acceptance of inputs. At an even higher level they may even be involved in redefinition of work goals. Proceeding to a higher level of autonomy at one and the same time involves the group more deeply in the longer range concerns of the company (e.g. product development, selection, training) and increases the autonomy that is possible at lower levels. Thus, regarding the latter, involvement in product specification can be associated with innovations in tooling up, staffing, training and also in work practices. Involvement in starting conditions may have a considerable effect on the methods of work that they can choose.

People cannot be expected to accept responsibility for production, as a group, unless a number of conditions are met. The psychological requirements that an individual worker has of his job are just about equally relevant for a face-to-face group of workers. They must know that they can aim at targets that are explicit, realistic and challenging to them; and they must have a feedback of group performance.

In setting and agreeing targets care must be taken to avoid lopsided simple minded targets that might encourage shoddy workmanship, unsafe practices or a 'bullgang' atmosphere where group members come under pressure to go for target levels that are only really suitable for the young, the strong and the greedy.

They must feel that the membership of their group is to some degree under their control. They must furthermore feel that how their leadership is organised is their business. Naturally, group integration will be low unless there is sufficient multi-skilling to allow flexible allocation of work within the group, to both individuals and sub-groups. How they allocate the work should be their responsibility, with explicitly agreed limitations to protect plant, safety etc.

It will be noted that these steps toward setting up autonomous work groups requires more explication of goals, methods and responsibilities than is usual. The commonsense and intuitive judgement of a supervisor is no longer enough. However, if these things are not worked out there is a danger of drifting into a laissez-faire atmosphere. The laissez-faire group is not autocratic but is certainly not democratic.

This is not a minor point. We have not been talking about simply removing autocratic controls and letting people find their own natural way of doing things. The alternative we are presenting is that of democratic control, not laissez-faire; a larger degree of self-management but management for all that. It is also not a recommendation to return to something like the cottage industry system that preceded the factory system. Modern industry, commerce and administration requires much closer managerial controls in order to justify the release of people from work by greater use of machinery and plant. That is, we are suggesting that better management is required and that more self-management is better management.

A modified form. The alternative organisation discussed above implies that a fair degree of multi-skilling is possible and hence that people can make real decisions about the switching of jobs. However, there are important areas of work where multi-skilling is not feasible. In research and development projects one may have to have such diverse skills as mathematical statisticians, chemists, economists. Each has his own special contribution to make and while the overall success of the project depends on the effective co-ordination of their activities one cannot expect to achieve this along the path of each person becoming expert in all of the required disciplines. In the management of enterprises we confront the same dilemma.

Beneath the managing director are usually functional managers for such things as production, finance, marketing, personnel and administration, R & D. They are typically chosen for their expertise and it is not expected that the production manager will be as good at financial matters as the finance manager. They in turn expect to be judged and rewarded for their expertise in their function.

Organised bureaucratically these work sections show the same shortcomings as are described above. Concern about this has been manifested in the rash of efforts at 'matrix' and 'project' organisations for R & D work and 'team building' for management. A lot of these efforts have been described as creating pockets within persisting bureaucratic structures where there is an 'open culture', 'trust' and 'understanding'. In many ways they seem like laissez-faire policies to let special kinds of people 'do their own thing in their own way.'

A more prosaic but effective solution is along the lines of the principle discussed in connection with multi-skilled autonomous groups: *locating responsibility for co-ordination clearly and firmly with those whose efforts require co-ordination if the common objectives are to be achieved.*

The change we are proposing can be represented diagrammatically as follows, using the management example:

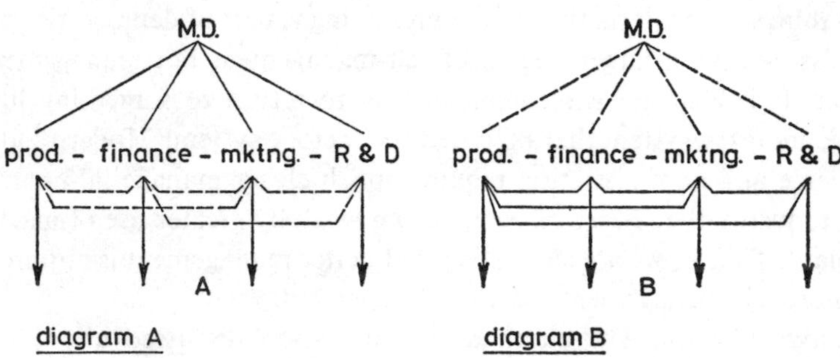

diagram A diagram B

In the normal bureaucratic state (diagram A) the functional managers will be primarily jockeying for influence with the MD so that he comes down in favour of their functional policies. This does not exclude temporary informal alliances between some functional managers to better ward off the threats of others. All rather suggestive of palace politics.

In the team concept (diagram B) the functional manager is judged and rewarded, or punished, as much for his effective co-ordination as for his ability to propose and implement policies in his division of the organisation. If an unresolved conflict arises between his managers the M.D. must sort out whether it is because one or more of them is incapable or unwilling to find a suitable compromise or whether the framework of policy that he is responsible for creating is inadequate. In the first case he must decide on some re-education or re-deployment; in the second, he must move from the normal operating mode, where he is relatively free from ongoing intra-organisational commitments, into a policy forming mode. He and his managers need remain in the 'policy mode' only long enough to create an adequate framework of operating policies. I have been inclined in the past to write off the style adopted in the policy mode as rather irrelevant; M.D.'s form a very small proportion of the work force! This now seems an unfair reflection of my experience. Admittedly, a relevant and acceptable body of overall policy must come into being, no matter how. However, an M.D. who denies to his managers involvement in formulating the principles they must use to co-ordinate their efforts must be dangerously conceited or charismatic.

Respecifying job responsibilities in line with diagram B would seem to be a simple matter. In fact, it seems from my experience, that only time and a few unpleasant but exemplary experiences are needed before the changed nature of managerial (or project team) responsibilities is grasped. More difficult is the transition to and for the 'policy forming mode.' If this is too frequent the 'time span of responsibility' of managers or researchers can be so reduced that they are, once again, just cogs. If it is to be as infrequent as possible and yet adequately reflect the rate of change in the organisation's environment objectives, resourches, then the team will have to adopt means of joint exploration and search that are not now commonly used.

A final point should be made about this modified design. This is with regard to the emergence of leadership. (A problem that is not quite so pressing at the occupational level where multi-skilling is feasible; at least not until it is realised that the royal road to management is not necessarily through prior tertiary education.) The bureaucratic system (diagram A) makes it very difficult to identify a potential leader. Is the next M.D. or project leader to be a man who was just so good (or lucky) at his specialist contribution that he put his colleagues in the shade? Is such a man the one best fitted to ensure the overall objective? This is difficult to know in the type of organisation where a person is paid for putting his best effort into his speciality.

In a genuine team structure (diagram B) it is relatively easier to see who is best capable of grasping the overall structure within which he better makes his specialist contribution. It may be for example the production manager who recognises that he must accept a sub-optimal solution to the length of his production runs if marketing requires a greater range of products; to accept a sub-optimal level of stocks with all the difficulties it makes for managing his production if the company needs a higher level of liquidity. It is the ability to work in this way that would indicate a potential for overall leadership.

If groups of men are to be expected to take responsibilities for production it is highly desirable that they feel they have taken a real part in designing what they are going to do. For many years, particularly in Norway, we felt that this involvement needed only their right to choice in matters of detail, a genuine democratic vote by them as whether to go into the new scheme of working and real guarantees about their right to opt out, individually and collectively. We have learnt that this creates an unhealthy reliance on outside experts and hinders the emergence of a self sustaining learning process in the groups. In the last couple of years in Australia we have found (particularly with ICI, Shell and the Commonwealth Public Service) that the most fruitful way to proceed is to involve workers and management in 2-3 day 'participative design workshops'. The aims of the design are spelt out to the participants as in the above statement of psychological requirements and they then proceed to:

1. analyse how the job is now done
2. assess how far this falls short of meeting the human requirements
3. redesign for a better way of doing the job (if such is felt to be needed)
4. work out how the new design could be implemented.

Part II: Participative Design Workshops – a description

The role played by social scientists in these workshops is much more congruent with the philosophy and ideals of participative democracy than was the earlier role. This is brought out most clearly by the ways in which analysis is handled, the involvement of relevant workers in the process itself and the resource role of the external agent. The learning environment created in these workshops is therefore itself a working example of the democratic model of organisational structure.

The basic assumption underlying the methods described here is that the most adequate and effective designs come from those whose jobs are under review. It is only from people pooling their various and usually fragmented, but always detailed, knowledge that a comprehensive and relatively stable design can come. More than that, it is only when the people involved work out their own designs that the necessary motivation, responsibility and commitment to effective implementation is present. The difficulties which are almost inevitably met in the initial phases of implementation may be found to be overwhelming if designs are imposed from above or by external agencies such as social scientists. The people must own their section of the organisation if they are to take responsibility for it.

As will become obvious from the following discussions the philosophy of participation as spelt out in practical detail is considered appropriate not only to industrial and white collar/clerical work sites but also to community designs and functions.

The time allotted to these workshops is usually one and a half to three days. Programing after the first three or so working sessions should remain open to capitalise on group tempo, need for major issues to be discussed in plenary session, etc.

Selection of persons to be involved in design

Generally the most important criterion to be observed is the size of the design group.

1. Given a small discrete or well defined section or unit, say 4-10 persons, it is best that everybody in that unit work together on the design. The size of the group will be increased of course by the desirable, if not necessary, inclusion of union representatives, first line supervisors and other management personnel representing critical interfaces. The size of the group may be increased in this situation if the people already have established close social or work relationships, or if it is a well delineated section – the personnel section. Department of Overseas Trade with 15 persons functioned well as a total design group.
2. Given a large unit, such as an assembly line it is necessary to ask the personnel of this unit to select an appropriate number of its members to do the design. Guidelines for this choice should be outlined in terms of the principles of the 'deep slice', that is a slice through the hierarchy of the organisation from shop floor to relevant management functions.

The 'deep slice' was used as a strategic technique for the first time in Australia in 1971. It was tried as a response to a receptive and antiexpert oriented climate where the demand for visible and self generating change was strong. This climate and awareness of the need for change with its attendent sense of urgency would appear to be another of the factors leading to this further democratisation of workshop design.

In the case of SAMCOR[2] the Yearling Beef Hall selected as its deep slice 2 labourers, 2 slaughtermen, the rover and the floater (first line supervisors for slaughtermen and labourers respectively), the boardwalker (superintendent of the Yearling Hall), and the fitter. Present also for part of the time were the secretary of the Meat Workers Union, the General Manager of SAMCOR and the worker director of the Board. One each of the labourers and slaughtermen were union delegates on the floor.

It is obviously not a feasible alternative to have separate groups working on part solutions or aspects of a design.

One special contingency needs to be mentioned. It has been found to be highly disruptive of groups in the design process if latecomers are perm-

2. South Australian Meat Corporation.

itted to join without the experience of the initial briefing. This briefing must be replicated for latecomers if they are to work constructively on the design.

Participation of union representatives and foremen

The same comments on ownership and understanding of design criteria and their implications apply to both union representatives and foremen/supervisors.

1. In the case of unions it is necessary that they are present to safeguard existing awards and agreements concerning all aspects of the job;
2. understand the role of demarcations in multi-skilled group functions and then to participate in possible future discussions as to ways of rationalising both demarcations and skill barriers;
3. see democratisation as a further benefit to the shop floor or operator level and ways in which unions can enlarge their sphere of negotiation with management to include this further benefit.

For foremen participation is essential. A foreman will often be the most experienced member of the design team. He has the experience therefore to help:

1. identify the extent and the boundaries of the natural working group;
2. realise training requirements for members of the group;
3. spell out his role either
   a. as most experienced or trainer member of the group or
   b. as the boundary rider of the group or groups with special responsibility for planning input/output schedules or intergroup links.

His participation in solving questions of this nature will help to ensure that his relinquishment of his previous functions of direct control and co-ordination will be smooth and replaced by more effective relationships encouraged by mutual understanding. The process of mutual understanding and trust already begins in the life of the design team as it works as a group towards the common goal of 'more human jobs for all.'

Participation of other managers

It is assumed that the sanction, approval and understanding of consequences of top management have been assured before the event of the seminar. However;

1. this understanding in particular will be furthered if management can participate in the design process itself, at beginning and end.
2. Any remaining suspicions of union and operators will be further alleviated if management in person can, at the time of the workshop, reiterate either by word or deed its encouragment of the purposes of the design team. Management should not be present throughout the process except perhaps as observer but they should be encouraged to come in at the beginning to state organisational goals and at the end to explicitly judge whether organizational goals are being well served.
3. Management better appreciate the organisational implications, e.g. training requirements and possible costs thereof, manpower situation, recruitment strategies, etc. if they can drop in towards the end to hear the team sum up their design efforts.

The outside expert

In these workshops it is *not* necessary that the outsiders are experts in the field of work that is being designed. Their job is to help the assembled worker and management pool their knowledge and use their expertise, wisdom and brains. This does entail enough familiarity with the work in question to follow the discussions and sense when bottlenecks are emerging, red herrings being pursued or when pseudo obstacles or conflicts are being generated (it is remarkable to find in any workplace how many things are technically impossible; things that have been done 'in the place next door' for years). But this role is a long way from that of the expert who presents the best solutions.

An outsider is relevant simply as *facilitator and external resource*. As a facilitator he can umpire, suggest, criticise. As an external resource he can help broaden the workshop's range of experience and deepen their analysis with social scientific concepts.

Briefly his various responsibilities fall into the areas of:

Introduction
Method of analysis
Process and content resource for group
Implementation

1. Introduction

The basic content of the introduction is contained in Part I of this Appendix. Presentation of this content appears to be most effective when it is simple, brief and visual. It is infrequent that further clarification of basic concepts is requested. They seem to be readily grasped regardless of the educational level of the participants.

2. Method of analysis

The following method is best introduced immediately after questions about basic concepts and before the group begins to work autonomously on the task of design or redesign.

The design team is asked firstly to draw up a simple table such as Figure 3. On this they are asked to rate *every* job or skill grouping required by the section task as it stands at the moment.

Figure 3. Example of first stage analysis. Class of job or skill grouping.

		Typists Clerks	Filing	Receptionist	Accountant etc.
Psychological criteria	Decision making	2	1	7	9
	Variety optimal	4	2	5	6
	Learning	2	1	6	8
	Mutual Support and Respect	3	3	0	0
	Meaningfulness	3	1	5	7
	Desirable Future	4	2	2	9

The team may prefer if time is short to estimate the criteria for each job on a (—, 0, +) scale indicating insufficient, adequate, ample on each criteria. However, even if time is not a priority the team should be reminded that the ratings from 0-10 are only to give estimated relativities for quality of job between section colleagues and that the more important task of resesign will be more time consuming.

The advantages of this first analysis are firstly that any misconceptions of the nature of criteria are hammered out by the group and a common and well founded understanding is established. Secondly, this first task is usually sufficient for members of the team to become acquainted with each other if they have not worked together closely on site, and to work through first stages of group formation. This is usually found to be necessary sooner or later because of the fragmentation that exists on the job. (A cohesive work group is formed fairly fast under these circumstances where involvement with such a personally important task as the organisation of one's own job is very high.)

Once the first stage analysis is completed to the group's satisfaction they should begin to look at the work process flows through the section or unit to gain an appreciation of degrees of interdependencies, inbalances and the length/size of total task leading to final product(s).

Within this analysis process stages should be assessed in terms of training or skilling requirements, and any natural breaks in the process or flow should be noted in case the section should need to be divided into more than one semi-autonomous group.

The group often finds it useful to set up a skilling table such as Figure 4 to help assess future training needs if multi-skilling is not adequate at the moment to allow semi-autonomous group function.

Figure 4. **Multi-skilling table.**

		Skills required for group task				Number
		J	K	L	M	of skills
Individuals in the group	Mary	x		x		2
	Jim	x	x	x		3
	John	x			x	2
	Alice	x				1
	Joe	x	x	x	x	4
	Jenny	x				1
	Number with skill	6	2	3	2	

In the example given in Figure 4 it is obvious that Alice and Jenny would be unable to replace any others in an emergency, or rotate to gain variety in job. Also skills K and M can only be handled by two individiduals which may inhibit flexible manning. Although it is rarely essential that there be complete multi-skilling in a group there should be sufficient flexibility built into the group to cope with absentees and the extremes of fluctuation in work load at any stage of the work flow.

After the group has completed a design for the unit it is often useful to return to the first stage of the analysis and check that no particular jobs have been left out of consideration in the new structure.

3. Resource for group

It is essential that the facilitator act only as a resource person after he has given the introduction. *This is best done by leaving the group to work alone.* He may be close at hand in the case of no consensus of meaning within the group on a particular issue and he may return to work with the group after its initial settling and formation stages. Or he may in fact not be needed until the group is ready to discuss its interim or final design.

As well as ensuring the formation of a work group this behaviour of the facilitator has indirect learning for the group. Whether or not this is made explicit, the members of the design team now have at least one experience of an autonomous group who has successfully worked towards its task goal. It is useful to point this out to members who become resistant to the idea of groups functioning without constant supervision or get carried away on the myth, that a 'natural boss' always emerges in response to 'natural dependency needs'.

It is rare that the resource person is required to deal directly with technological queries. The resource may have to inquire into the technology on his own initiative if for some reason work is blocked or analysis shows results which are clearly unrealistic. Often it is useful to be able to cite examples of the same or similar technologies.

There are other times that a resource may need to intervene. One group of managers and unionists interpreted mutual support as a craftsman having an unskilled offsider to fetch and carry tools, etc. for him. (Such an example is however unusual.) More usual is the case where a particularly happy set of interpersonal relations is accepted as a substitute for the democratic structure.

The design team may often on their first attempt bring up a design which is incomplete or an example of limited individual job enrichment rather than democratisation. In the case of an incomplete design it is worthwhile questioning whether it is a simple case of incompleteness or due to such factors as union demarcations.

If a group returns a typical individual enrichment design the implications are often quickly cleared by reverting to explanation of these via the visual structural modules. There is a case where blocks to democratisation may be very real. This involves a group's inability to deal with the new role of first line supervisors. If a significant segment of a plant or office, etc., is to be redesigned it is estimated that only about one third of existing supervision positions will be necessary after democratisation. As guarantees of no retrenchment are often demanded the resettlement of this remaining two thirds of existing supervisors requires a searching and creative problem solving process. In the time available for discussion of such matters it is often the only way to extract agreements that after retirement of present individuals no further replacement will occur. The groups then may be granted their real decision making powers in the hope that relations between the groups and their short term supervisors will be sorted out in the process of implementation.

4. Implementation – discussion of designs at the time of finalising designs
The following issues commonly arise. They are not discussed in any order of priority.

1. Sharing the increased productivity. After the initial protected period of settling down into a new work organisation some increase in productivity usually results. It is the joint responsibility of managements and unions to anticipate this increase and prepare to negotiate new agreements for sharing when the new rate of productivity becomes stable. It is one of the responsibilities of management that be made clear at the start.

2. Regular reviews of flat rate awards have been found preferable to incentive bonus payments, even on a group payment basis. Where bonuses have been traditional it is still preferable to institute regular re-negotiation and maintain bonuses only at a nominal or symbolic level. Individual incentives are almost impossible to allocate within the framework of semi autonomous groups and group bonuses become difficult when there are strong interdependencies between the tasks of groups in a complex plant.

3. Training costs may increase significantly in some technologies. This is a spread de-skilling of the work-force has been one of the results of so-called where this is not already in effect. Members of multi-skilled groups are paid to the highest level of skill they hold although this skill may not be in constant use. It is to the advantage of management to use this scheme as it helps to ensure that the benefits of multi-skilling will be retained. Widespread de-skilling of the work-force has been one of the results of so-called Scientific Management. (And the community picks up the tab with national re-training schemes.)

4. Composition of the group. A group may fail to cohere or reach its goals if it is lacking initially in sufficient experienced members to provide leader-

ship. As well as experience with the technology there needs to be some members with the maturity to guide the group to effective autonomy. This often means keeping the group together to its appointed task in the face of distractions caused by short term individual needs.

5. Selection of group members. Established working groups must be allowed some say in the composition of the group. This can be arranged in terms of a trial period for new members after choice from a short list prepared by management. Incompatibility of individuals with groups is often simply resolved by the individual choosing to look elsewhere for a more appropriate work culture.

6. Loners can usually be accommodated by groups by designing around them. The special case of the loner who has difficulty in adapting to democratic ways after years of entrenched status differentiations often needs the consultation of the group and management. In extreme examples of sabotage of the groups efforts, management may need to consider horizontal displacement of the individual concerned.

This is an example of the many ways in which management must be prepared to be supportive of groups, particularly in the early stages of implementation.

7. Goal setting. It is essential that the task goals set jointly by management and the groups be compounded both of task (quantity and quality) and human components. Where the goals set are only targets of quantity the opportunity is opened of subversion of the group into a 'gang'. The incomplete nature of the goal leads directly to intergroup competition, neglect of interdependencies of group tasks and abuse of individual members – their needs and unique contributions.

8. Leaders and spokesmen. It is unusual for a well functioning group to show a constant pattern of leadership. In the true sense of leaderless group – a group of leaders – the leadership function will move from person to person as the progression of the task demands differing experiences and skills. However, it has often been found useful for the group to nominate a spokesman to operate intermittently at the boundaries of the group. This is not necessarily a leadership function except in the minor sense that communications through the spokesman are effective to the extent that they are accurate and representative.

9. Autonomy and semi-autonomy. It may sometimes happen that while goal setting has been a joint task of groups and management and the contract of the group is for semi-autonomy in terms of its function within the total framework of company policy, industrial agreement, etc. a highly effective and successful group may gradually move to autonomy. The basis for this move is the over confidence of the group and its tight supporting infrastructure. The results are first noticed usually in a growing disregard for established safety procedures. It is the responsibility of the linkman or boundary rider to reaffirm the initially agreed limits to group function and responsibility, in consultation with other levels of management if necessary.

10. Training for Linkmen/Boundary Riders. When the initial problems relating to either relocation, retirement of first line supervisors have been solved the question remains whether those chosen as linkmen have the necessary experience or training to carry out the new role. This new role, encompassing as it does oversight of intergroup relations and the flow of inputs/outputs, requires capacities which are strictly managerial rather than supervisory. This qualitative difference often makes necessary retraining as well as reorientation of outlook. Management should be prepared to face costs for training in these positions as well as those of multi-skilling operatives.

In Summary it should be restated that these are only a selection of the issues that arise in implementing change from bureaucracy to democracy. This discussion of them is drawn from the experiences of those who have worked towards successful implementation. The reader is reminded that 'credulous imitation' is infrequently a formula for success. Effective problem solving is more likely to be achieved by those involved in their own unique variant of circumstances, history and technology.

Literature

Churchman, C. W. and F. E. Emery: On various approaches to the study of organizations, in Lawrence, J. R. (ed.), *Operational research and the social sciences*, Tavistock, London, 1966.

Davis, L. E. *et al.*: Current job design criteria, *Journal of industrial engineering*, 1955, 6, 5-11.

Davis, L. E.: Toward a theory of job design, *Journal of industrial engineering*, 1957, 5, 19-23.

Emery, F. E.: Characteristics of socio-technical systems, *doc.* 527, Tavistock Institute, London, 1959.

Emery, F. E.: First progress report on conceptualization, *doc.* T67. Second progress report on conceptualization, *doc.* T125, Tavistock Institute, London, 1963.

Emery, F. E.: The next thirty years, *Human relations*, No. 20, 1967.

Emery, F. E.: Bureaucracy and beyond, *Organizational dynamics*, Winter, 1974, 3-13.

Emery, F. E. and M. Emery: *Participative design*, Centre for Continuing Education, ANU, Canberra, 1974.

Emery, F. E. *et al.*: *Futures we're in*, Centre for continuing education, ANU, Canberra, 1974.

Emery, F. E. and O. A. Oeser: *Information, decision and action*, Cambridge University Press, Melbourne, 1958.

Emery, F. E. and E. Thorsrud: *Form and content in industrial democracy*, Oslo University Press, Oslo, 1964. Tavistock, London, 1969.

Emery, F. E. and E. L. Trist: *Socio-technical systems*, in Emery, F. E., *Systems thinking*, Penguin, London, 1969.

Engelstad, P. H.: *Technologi og sosial forandring på arbeidsplassen*, Tanum, Oslo, 1970.

Gulowsen, J.: *Selvstyrte arbeidsgrupper*, Tanum, Oslo, 1971.

Gulowsen, J.: The Norwegian Participation Project. The Norsk Hydro Fertilizer Plant, *AI-Doc.*, Oslo, 1974.

Herbst, P. G.: *Socio-technical design*, Tavistock, London, 1974.

Herbst, P. G.: Some reflections on the work democratization project, AI-Doc. 13/1974. To be published as part of a book: *Alternatives to hierarchies*, Nijhoff, Leiden, 1976.

Hill, P.: *Toward a new philosophy of management*, Gower Press, London, 1974.

Jaques, E.: *The Changing Culture of Factory*, Tavistock/Routledge, London, 1951.

Jenkins, D.: *Job power*, Doubleday, N.Y., 1973.

Jordan, N.: *Themes in speculative psychology*, Tavistock, London, 1968.

Lewin, K. *et al.*: Patterns of aggressive behaviour in experimentally created 'social climates', *Journal of social psychology*, 1939, 10, 271-299.

Mann, F.: Studying and Creating Change. *Industrial Relations Research Publications* No. 17, N.Y., 1957.

Mann, F. and R. Hoffman: *Automation and the worker*, Holt, Rinehart and Winston, New York, 1960.

Marek, J. *et al.*: Report 1. Industrial Democracy Project. The Wire Drawing Mill of Christiania Spigerverk. IFIM, Trondheim, 1964.

McGregor, D.: *The Human Side of Enterprise*, McGraw Hill, N.Y., 1960.

Mumford, L.: *The myth of the machine*, Secker Warburg, London, 1967.

O'Toole, J. *et al.*: *Work in America*, M.I.T. Press, Cambridge Mass., 1973.

Rice, A. K.: *Productivity and social organization*, Tavistock, London, 1958.

Roggema, J. and E. Thorsrud: *Et skip i utvikling*, Tanum, Oslo, 1974.

Selznick, P.: *Leadership in administration*, Row Peterson, Evanston Ill., 1957.

Thorsrud, E. and F. E. Emery: *Industrielt demokrati*, Universitetsforlaget, Oslo, 1964.

Thorsrud, E. and F. E. Emery: *Mot en ny bedriftsorganisasjon*, Tanum, Oslo, 1970.

Trist, E.: Human Relations in Industry, Paper to Vienna seminar under the auspices of the Congress for Cultural Freedom, 1958.

Trist, E. L. and K. Bamforth: Social and psychological consequences of the Longell method of coal-getting, *Human relations*, 1951, 4, 3-38.

Trist, E. L. *et al.*: *Organizational choice*, Tavistock, London, 1963.

Work Research Institutes (WRI), Occational Papers (*AI-Doc.*) 23/1973 (Blichfeldt): Organizational Change as the Development of Networks and Mutual Trust, Oslo 1973.